MAESTÀ P

PARANORMAL STORIES

VERITAS VOS LIBERABIT

CONTENTS.

Introduction 5

Chapter I. Temet Nosce 7

I.1. The Construct 9
I.2. Paranormal Phenomena 16
I.3. Ghost Sories 29
I.4. The Desert of the Real 39
I.5. Density and Dimensions 42
I.6. The Planetary Energy Network 47

Chapter II. My experiences 61

II.1. My Near-Death Experiences 63
II.2. Extraterrestrial Phenomena 67
II.3. Strange Dreams 74

Chapter III. Paranormal Compendium 77

III.1. Divine Punishment 79
III.2. The Cries of Damned Souls 82
III.3. The Mummy of Ramesses II 85
III.4. The Legendary Photo of the Djinn 90
III.5. Mary Toft, the rabbit women 93
III.6. The President's Premonitory Dreams 97
III.7. Gustav Jung's Synchonicities 102
III.8. The Human Pair 109
III.9. Peter Sellers' out-of-body experience 112
III.10. Haray, Berlitz out-of-body experiences 114

III.11. Joseph Figlock and the Baby 118
III.12. The Cursed Chamber 120
III.13. Springer's Brothers 122
III.14. Back to the Future. 124
III.15. A Love story 126
III.16. Final Destination 129
III.17. Roy Sullivan, «the lightning» 132
III.18. Premonition 135
III.19. Normandy landings 139
III.20. Goodbye ! 142
III.21. The Ghost train 145
III.22. The Premonitory Dream 147
III.23. A Loyal Master 150
III.24. Criminal Investigation, Reincarnation . . 153
III.25. Abduction and UFO Hunting 156
III.26. Norfolk Regiment 164
III.27. Archaeological excavation in Tarsus 166
III.28. The Montauk Project 183

Sources 224

INTRODUCTION.

The book that you are about to read is a collection of paranormal stories and anecdotes, but before getting to the heart of the matter, we must first determine the framework in which we evolve. To talk about paranormal, we must first understand what "normal" is.

By definition, normal means:
that meets the standard, the standard, or is consistent with what we think is fair and equitable. In other words, if the majority of humans are wrong, then the norm will be a mistake, and those who dare to go against this mistake, will be considered abnormal, heretical or conspiratorial.

Considering only this aspect, we can easily deduce, that the normal can in no case be considered as the absolute truth, or if we push the reflection a little further, the normal would not even be reality. The normal could claim, at most, to be a tiny part of reality.

You will find that some of these stories are crude hoaxes that many have believed, these false stories have gone around the world and no doubt will continue to do so, we will continue with several anecdotes from my personal experience, and we'll end with a collection of global paranormal stories. These magical stories are real winks that the matrix addresses us, they continue to make us dream, they are like a glimmer of hope in a world that seems to have locked the majority of the consciences that it hosts. I wish you a good reading.

Maestà Pastore.

I. TEMET NOSCE.

"If all physical, chemical and biological phenomena beyond our comprehension were to be called supernatural, there would hardly be anything but supernatural in the world"

> Gustave Le Bon.

I.1. THE CONSTRUCT.

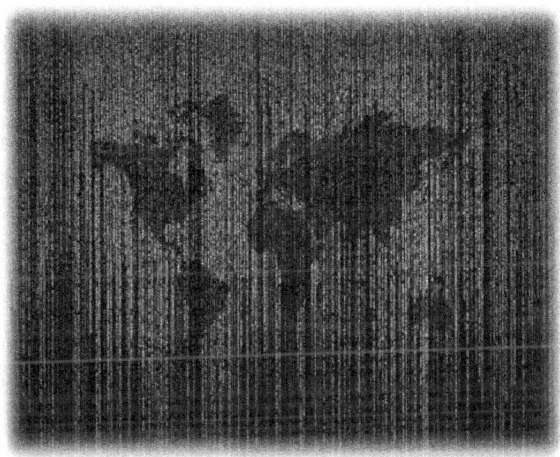

Perhaps the truth escapes us, because we do not understand our environment and without first having understood the structure in which we evolve, we cannot speak of normal, abnormal, paranormal or even real. In this chapter, we will discuss topics such as the storage and dissemination of information, the atom, energy frequencies, waves, different densities of vibrations and dimensions, that is to say all that make up our reality.

We will continue with paranormal phenomena, we will try to define and understand them. The purpose of this part of the book will be to allow readers to qualify paranormal stories and anecdotes. It is for this reason that the different points of this part will not be deepened, but rather flown over.

Let's start with the storage and dissemination of information and let's try together to understand why our Universe functions as a three-dimensional hologram.

It's the 1940s and it all starts with a simple question, asked by the American neurophysiologist Karl Pribram. Pribram wonders "in what part of the brain would memories be stored? ".

Until then, the dominant idea was that memories would be stored in a specific place in the brain. This belief was based on the work of Canadian neurosurgeon Wilder Penfield from 1920. Penfield, by electrically stimulating the temporal lobe of some of his patients, managed to bring back their buried memories.

In 1946, Pribram met neuropsychologist Karl Lashley, the two men worked together at the laboratory of the Yerkes National Primate Research Center in Atlanta, and then in Florida at Orange Park. This meeting will be decisive for Pribram because Karl Lashley had to his credit experiences going against those of Penfield.

These experiments could easily change the dominant idea of the 1940s; unlike Penfield, Lashley argued that memories or all information processed by the brain, were managed simultaneously by the whole of it. For example, in one of his many experiments, Lashley operated the brains of rats placed in a maze, systematically removing a portion of their brain and then observing these guinea pigs who continued to perform the tasks for which they were previously trained.
No matter what part of the brain was taken away from the rats, the rats, without exception, still managed to perform their tasks, sometimes very slowly, sometimes by limping, sometimes by dragging, but they still managed, other experiments on other animals gave similar results. Despite so much evidence in his favour, Lashley was unable to explain how his theory worked.

In 1948 Pribram, after accepting an offer from Yale University, separated from Lashley. For more than 12 years, the neurophysiologist continued to be obsessed with Lashley's idea, without being able to provide an answer. In the mid-1960s, reading an article in the magazine "Scientific American" describing the operation of the first hologram, Pribram stumbled upon the solution of his problem.

To understand Pribram's illumination, we must first explain how a hologram works:
A holographic image is obtained by dividing a single beam of pure light (a laser) into two separate beams. The first bounces on the object to reproduce. The second, routed by a set of mirrors, collides with the diffracted lightwaves of the first. The result is a system of interference fringes that will register on a photosensitive emulsion. But, unlike what happens in photography, all the information is recorded on each fragment of the medium. Even if you break a holographic plate into a thousand pieces, each fragment can be used to reconstruct the entire image. Let us suppose that the image projected on the holographic plate was that of an apple, once the plate is broken and the ray directed at any fragment of the plate, of it, will emanate the holographic image of the whole apple. An apple of reduced size, but whole.

It is this last aspect that fascinated Pribram, because he saw there a metaphor of the mode of distribution of memories in the brain, which shelters in each of its parts, enough to rebuild a memory in its entirety.
The brain therefore functions like a hologram, it is able to store huge amounts of information in a very small space, just as a single cubic centimeter of holographic film can contain up to ten billion bits of information.

This fundamental discovery would soon pale in comparison to what Pribram would discover by consulting the work of physicist David Bohm. If Pribram, with his theory, could prove that the brain functioned like a hologram, Bohm him with his "theory of the implicit order" transposed the same idea on the whole Universe. According to this theory, a deeper reality underlies the Universe, and the world that we perceive with our senses is only an illusion, a kind of ghost or projection of this hidden coherence. The notion of implicit order emphasizes the primacy of structure and process over individual objects. The latter are interpreted as simple approximations of an underlying dynamic system. The implicit order is therefore a hyper-dimensional reality that governs the world of matter, it is the very seat of consciousness and all the phenomena related to it.

Bohm's theory with its hyperdimensional aspect joins the representation of the Universe in "flat square torus" of the famous mathematician John Nash, and has potentially all the arguments that would explain paranormal phenomena such as synchronicity, clairvoyance, distance vision, telepathy, psychokinesis or lucid dreaming, the impression of déjà vu, imminent death experiences, astral travel...

But in this case, how can we define the real? According to Bohm's theory, the world we perceive with our senses is only an illusion, therefore a kind of projection of a hidden coherence. We find the same theory in the film "The Matrix" by the Wachowski brothers. Morpheus questions Neo about the real: " What is the real? What is your definition of reality? If you want to talk about what you can touch, what you can taste, see and feel, then reality is only an electrical signal interpreted by your brain".

We can confirm what Morpheus is saying with the following experiment:

The subject hypnotized by the hypnotherapist, is warned by the latter that his arm will soon be subjected to a burning iron. Then the hypnotherapist, using his two fingers, applies pressure on the arm of his subject. After this pressure, the subject's arm shows a trace of burning followed by blistering. We know that the blister is a defense mechanism against chemical, physical or microbial aggression of the skin. In this experiment the skin of the subject, although exposed to no aggression, has exactly the same characteristics as that of a person who has been burned. For the blister, we can deduce that the brain under hypnosis simply interpreted information and triggered a defense mechanism, but for the burn trace this explanation is no longer credible. However, the burn trace is very real, which proves that what is called "reality" is only a series of electrical signals interpreted by our brain. So there may be a reality that is superimposed on our gaze to prevent us from seeing the truth and paranormal phenomena would be in this case winks, even evidence of this underlying reality.

I.2. PARANORMAL PHENOMENA.

Here, we will discuss topics such as lucid dreaming, dreaming in the dream, impression of déjà vu, near death experience, astral exit, synchronicity, premonitory dream and everything related to ghosts, spirits or jinns. At the risk of repeating myself, I would like to clarify once again that we should not be afraid of this kind of experience. We must interpret them with the awareness that we are constantly swimming in an ocean of energy frequencies, which is the result of a system spreading information like a hologram. And that all these experiences are only the interpretation by our brain of electrical signals and energetic frequencies.

THE DREAM.

The dream is defined as a series of psychic phenomena occurring during sleep. Scientists can detect, based on frequency variations, emitted by our brain, that we are passing from one sleep state to another and also dreaming, but can in no way detect whether the person is lucid during his dream or the dimensions explored by the spirit of it, because we are talking about that. When the mystics defined the dream as a walk of the soul through other worlds. In fact, they defined, in their own way, this relationship between the information stored in the matter that our mind travels, arbitrarily or not.

There are several types of dreams, some types of dreams can be easily explained by the overall state of the person. A healthy and sane person will dream of a walk along a beautiful river while a stressed and physically ill person will drown in the same river. We should not exclude those dreams that give us information about our general state, but this is not the case for all our dreams. There are dreams in which we are perfectly aware, there are others that seem so real to us, that once awakened, we ask questions about the very nature of "reality". It is this kind of dream that I would like to deepen, because it is those who betray this world of illusions.

THE DREAM WITHIN A DREAM.

Some specialists will speak here of exploration of the different layers of the unconscious, I prefer to define it as the exploration of the different states of consciousness or as the exploration of parallel dimensions through the mind. The first layer being the waking state, the dream state would therefore be the second layer and the dream in the dream the third, etc. Based on this scheme, we can easily place another state of consciousness, the state of zero consciousness or the state of absolute consciousness. A state that we could only reach by modifying our frequency, our vibration to emancipate ourselves from this prison in 3D. This might sound crazy to the uninitiated, but know that many experiments have been conducted in this area and continue to be. For example, during the Cold War, both American and Russian had a unit of extrasensory spies. These people were trained in remote vision and used for various spy tasks. I don't think they were disbanded after the Cold War.

THE LUCID DREAM.

This is another form of dream that science is struggling to explain to us. Lucid dreaming is, as its name suggests, a dream in which the subject is conscious of dreaming. Not to be confused with sleepwalking.

And when we are conscious of dreaming, we indulge in all kinds of fantasies, fly, cross walls, transform, spit fire... The possibilities are endless and our only limit is our imagination.

There are different techniques to help people who want to master this art, make their room warmer, take a hot bath before sleeping, turn off electronic devices, techniques to recognize the dream through reality tests... all the better if these techniques help some people to be masters of their dreams. I do not use any technique and I think that the simple will is enough to be lucid during a dream. Every time I fall asleep, I do it with the intention of wanting to control my dream, and that is enough. During my last lucid dream, I flew through the air and through walls.

In a lucid dream everything becomes possible for the subject once he realizes that he is dreaming, but until this click, the subject is master of nothing, he undergoes the reality of the dream, as we undergo the obstacles of our daily reality.

I think that lucid dreaming as the dream of false awakening could make us aware of the illusion of reality and allow us to awaken to mindfulness.

THE IMPRESSION OF DÉJÀ-VU.
(ALREADY SEEN)

All attempts to explain this phenomenon are only suppositions and hypotheses, because it cannot be measured, impossible indeed, to take a sample of people and wait for them to experience déjà vu. The phenomenon happens unexpectedly.

It goes without saying, the impression of déjà vu is a neurological phenomenon, the reception of information and its transformation know for a thousandth of a second a synchronization problem. A synchronization problem with what our brain interprets as our reality. Because it is the brain of the receiver that determines the nature of reality. It can therefore be multiple since it is subject to the subjective interpretation of each brain.
We can have several kinds of déjà-vu: the already-lived, the already-visited and the already-felt.

THE ALREADY LIVED.

You are in your living room, a door opens, a person enters and you have the strange feeling of having already experienced this scene.

We can explain it as a bug in the system that disseminates the information, that underlying system or the matrix if you prefer. This system is very old, begins to weaken and sometimes shows signs of weakness that are perceived as flash. This may also be due to a system update that sometimes some people might observe. The phenomenon is mainly observed in adolescents, because their brains are not yet fully conditioned, are open to all kinds of learning, including that of emancipating from the system.

THE ALREADY FELT.

It is a feeling of having already felt, another time, exactly the same as what we are feeling. So, it would be an emotional déjà vu. For example, you visit a place and you feel anxious, you may be visiting an old crime scene.

THE ALREADY VISITED.

It is the impression of having already visited a place that we discover for the first time.

If the impression of the already lived can be explained by a «bug» or an update made by the matrix, the already felt and the already visited could be explained, as manifestations of feeling coming from our previous lives.

THE ASTRAL PROJECTION.

Astral projection, also called astral travel, astral exit or out-of-body experience, is the act of dissociating one's body from what most religions and other esoteric beliefs call the soul, mind or consciousness. Here, our physical body would only be a temporary envelope of our true substance.
This substance that can be defined as mind, consciousness or soul can during an astral travel experience come out of the physical body and travel. As for the lucid dream all kinds of techniques exist to carry out this experiment, only a major difference is observed between the two events.
During a lucid dream the mind travels through another, or even several other dimensions, while during the astral journey it explores the same dimension as that of the physical body.

I had the chance to experience these two facts and I can assure you that the feeling is totally different. In the lucid dream you know that you are dreaming, it provides some comfort, you are confident and begin to experience all kinds of things of which you are the only virtuoso. In an astral travel experience the feeling is totally different. You feel like sucking up, as if your true self, your substance, your soul or spirit, were taken away from you. I had to interrupt the process several times right then and there, so terrifying. I have rarely passed the stage of aspiration, but many others have, here is the story of one of them.

Robert Monroe (1915-1995) is an American businessman and sound engineer, his first astral projection will be accidental.

The night of the events, Monroe, lying on his bed, was very happy, because for the first time in a very long time, he had no difficulty falling asleep. He fell asleep mentally planning his weekend, when he felt a jolt on his shoulder! Finding this strange, he opened his eyes and found himself with his nose glued, so that he first thought the floor of his room.

He then groped his shoulder and felt an unknown, cold object. He looked at it. It was the candlestick in his bedroom. Monroe then noticed with amazement that he was lying on the ceiling. Turning on himself, he looked up, and saw his bed, in which was his wife, and very close to her, a man with a mustache asleep. This set him off, and he took a determined step towards the ground to expel this stranger and at the same time plan his divorce.

When he finally realized that this man was none other than himself, in full sleep, astonished, panicked, he thought himself dead, he swam desperately towards his own body to reintegrate it, which he did quickly. Robert Monroe will not sleep that night.

This experience had such an impact on the businessman that he created the Monroe Institute in 1958. The Monroe Institute is a non-profit organization dedicated to the exploration of human consciousness.

Robert Monroe will repeat his out-of-body experiment many times, he will even develop a method called «hemispherical synchronization", allowing anyone to make an astral journey by listening to special sounds triggering a «binaural beat».

THE NEAR-DEATH EXPERIENCE.

Also known as NDE, the near-death experience refers to all sensations that follow a clinical death or advanced coma. Numerous studies are available on the subject, and it appears that between 2% and 18% of cardiac arrest victims experienced the NDE. These people relate more or less the same sensations, that is to say a out-of-body experience, the complete vision of one's own existence in a split second, the vision of a tunnel with a white light at the end of it, the impression of being enveloped by a white light, the encounter with spiritual entities or dead ancestors, a feeling of infinite love, peace and tranquility, the impression of an inexpressible experience and union with divine or supranormal principles, the impression of being liberated, to float and observe his physical body, some even describe the operating room of the hospital where doctors and nurses try to revive him. All these sensations are not experienced at the same time, nor by all people who have experienced an NDE, but we can easily deduce that many of them are during an NDE. You can find many accounts of near-death experience on the web, I had the chance to experience this fact, which I relate in the «My experiences» part of this book.

THE PREMONITORY DREAM AND SYNCHRONICITY.

The premonitory dream is a dream with a special character, in which the person is warned of upcoming and sometimes past events. These signs can be symbolic as in the dream of pharaoh in the bible. Genesis 41 -46.

Pharaoh said to Joseph, "In the dream, I was standing on the banks of the Nile, and seven cows were coming up from the Nile, fat and beautiful, grazing in the reeds.
Then, behind them, seven other cows rode, weak, very ugly and emaciated. I had never seen such ugliness in the whole country of Egypt.
The emaciated and ugly cows ate the first cows, the fat ones, which entered their belly. But we didn't realize that the fat people had got into their belly: they were as ugly as before. So, I woke up.

Here the prophet Joseph will interpret the dream and manage to organize the country in the face of the 7 years of drought represented here by the weak and emaciated cows, by storing enough food during the 7 years of abundance represented here by the 7 fat cows of Pharaoh's dream.

The signs can also be non-symbolic and more direct, like the vision of a future accident or other event of good or bad nature.

Synchronicity is a coincidence or a series of coincidences that suddenly make sense, it causes a strong emotion, it is a carrier of transformation and occurs at the right time. The best example is that of the Swiss psychiatrist Carl Gustav Jung and the golden beetle. Carl Gustav Jung is the creator of several concepts such as analytical psychology and synchronicity. For Jung, synchronicity reveals a union and continuity between the psychic and the physical.

The Story of the Golden scarab:

Carl Gustav Jung is in consultation with one of his patients who is going through a period of severe depression. Between her multiple problems, her patient tells her about the dream she had the day before. In his dream, a person offered him a golden scarab and strange thing as soon as the patient mentions the name of the insect he bumps against the window of the office. The psychiatrist then opens the window, grabs the insect, turns to the woman and says "there it is! Your golden scarab".

The golden scarab is a beetle called "Cetonia Aurata", the insect can be gray, copper, green or gold, but always metallic. The insect is present in central and southern Europe. But we agree that the European streets do not swarm.

Jung will interpret his patient's dream by explaining to him all the symbolism that revolves around this animal. Indeed, in ancient Egypt the golden beetle was the symbol of rebirth, of a second life. This event produces a shock in the mind of the patient, which allows her to heal.

Even if the premonitory dream and synchronicity are not systematically linked, the premonitory dream often precedes the phenomenon of synchronicity. To understand these two phenomena, it is imperative to change the way we interpret the notion of time and reality. Time is not something palpable, it has no physical reality in the Universe. It is we, Human, who at one point in our history, decided to facilitate our earthly actions, to divide and quantify the revolution of our planet around its star. So it's a psychological reality. The example of the golden beetle proves it, in this example, we are talking about retro-causality, that is to say, that there is a causal link, but a future event that is revealed to the patient in a dream she had in the past. If we accept that time is only an illusion, and that a part of us, our consciousness, is out of time, it suddenly makes these phenomena more acceptable

I.3. GHOST STORIES.

David Bohm's theory of "Implicate order and explicate order", the representation of the universe in flat square torus by mathematician John Nash, Karl Pribram's theory that the diffusion of information is similar to that of a holographic system, also have the ability to shed light on all these stories of ghosts, wandering spirits, angels, demons or djinns (in the East).

Once these theories are assimilated, ghost stories no longer scare us and become more acceptable, even harmless. As a reminder, the main idea of these theories is to make us understand, that information is not stored in the brain, but is present in any place and at any time.

So we are constantly swimming in an ocean of information that our brain interprets. Humans are like small antennae constantly interpreting past, present or future information. The majority of humans tuned to the same frequency throughout their lives, will live an anonymous and banal existence without even thinking about it, but others will have extraordinary experiences due to their clairvoyance, their curiosity, their gift and sometimes in the absence of this machine managing the implicit order that some call the matrix. The examples that will follow will allow us to better illustrate these theories.

Some mediums claim to see the future, others are supposedly capable of perceiving, by apparently supernatural means, the messages of the spirits of the deceased and of acting as intermediaries between the living and the dead, Still, others claim to collaborate with interdimensional entities, called "djinn" in the East. The truth is that few people have such gifts, and that this area abounds with charlatans taking advantage of the naivety of a generally uninformed population. Stefan Ossowiecki and George McMullen are not.

Stefan Ossowiecki is a Polish engineer with special skills from an early age. As a child, he will tell his mother that he sees colored bands encompassing the people he meets, which we can currently qualify as aura. He will be consulted by an ophthalmologist who will prescribe drops, later Ossowiecki will say that apart from having irritated his eyes his drops were of no use. The young boy will continue to see these bands of light around each person, but Ossowiecki's main gift was not to perceive a person's aura, but psychokinesis. His donation will be put to the test and then validated by two notable people. The first will be the parapsychologist and director of the international metapsychic institute Gustav Geley, the second will be the physiologist and Nobel laureate in medicine Robert Richet. It is 1935, in Warsaw, and the gift of Ossowiecki attracts the attention of the greatest ethnologist of the country Stanislaw Poniatowski.

Poniatowski tests Ossowiecki's gift by presenting him with prehistoric stones he had collected from various archaeological sites. The stones, essentially quartz, were shaped by the hand of man, but only the experts in the matter could differentiate them from a vulgar pebble. Each stone had been previously analyzed and dated by them, Poniatowski had these data in his notes and for the good progress of his experiment, hid them from the medium. Despite this, Ossowiecki will each time, surprisingly and giving a lot of details, situate the object in time, describe its environment, describe its former owner or owners, and the few times he contradicts the ethnologist's notes, after a second check, Poniatowski will be forced to admit that it was the medium that was right.

In one of his experiments, after coming into contact with a petrified piece of human foot, Ossowiecki will describe the following scene:

The colors of the room in which he found himself, gradually became pale, until the room itself became completely transparent, to give way to a scene from a very distant past. Ossowiecki found himself in the garden of a luxurious palace, before him, a young woman of a slightly tanned complexion. The woman was very beautiful and neat. She wore a white tunic, bracelets and various golden jewels, the medium could see under her crown decorated with multiple jewels her carefully woven black hair. She was a princess, she was married, her husband appeared, a skinny man with long woven hair, her face could be seen between the two strands that fell on her face. Then a series of scenes from the woman's life quickly challenged Ossowiecki. He finally saw the woman die in childbirth. One last scene showed the woman being mummified and her funeral.

Ossowiecki always proceeded in the same way, he took an object in hand and went into a state of trance, the room where he was, became transparent, the decor changed and the medium found itself viewing scenes from the past associated with the object. Many archaeological discoveries are to his credit in particular, he will be the first to assert that prehistoric men light themselves with oil lamps. We will find these famous lamps, similar to the description given by the medium, during the excavations of the archaeological site of the Dordogne in France.

Through these mediums practicing psychokinesis, archaeology had just discovered a new tool, which we will call intuitive archaeology.

At the beginning of the 20th century, the first to be identified as such was the architect and psychic researcher Frederick Bligh Bond. He led the excavations to restore the abbey of Glastonbury (England) in its initial plan.
Between 1931 and 1941, the collaboration between the medium Ossowiecki and the ethnologist Poniatowski followed, but the duo is not the only example in this matter.

We can also cite General James Scott Elliot, who in 1961 conducted research on the location of archaeological sites.

In 1970 in the USSR, the government funded the team led by Aleksandr Ivanovich Pluzhnikov. The team was tasked with intuitively searching for and describing the contours of underground architectural and historical objects that do not show up on the surface of the ground.

During the same period, in Canada, professor and archaeologist J.Norman Emerson will use the donations of Georges McMullen. Georges McMullen is a truck driver and like Ossowiecki, he had the ability to psychometrically relate to objects and use them to slip into scenes from the past, plus when McMullen was going to an archaeological site, he could immediately access the past. In one of these experiments, McMullen was on an archaeological site and hurried on all sides. When Emerson questioned him, McMullen replied that he was delineating the contours of an Iroquoian longhouse. After only six months, the house was dug up and exactly matched McMullen's description.

Being very skeptical of McMullen's donations before working with him, Emerson will say at a conference dedicated to archaeology:

'I am convinced that the information I transmitted on the archaeological facts and sites was obtained through a psychic person, for whom there is no evidence that he obtained it as a result of conscious reasoning. The capabilities of this medium have brought a new and holistic perspective to archaeology, and I believe that future work of using mediums in archaeological research should receive urgent priority. '

These examples allow us to better understand our environment which oscillates between the third and the fifth dimension. The next example will allow us to make the junction between our three-dimensional environment, and the one to which our universe really belongs, the fifth.
The idea that holographic recordings of the past, are recorded in the cosmic waves of the Universe and can be captured from time to time by the human mind, and reappearing as holograms can also explain some of the ghost stories in circulation. These ghosts can be three-dimensional holographic images of people or a scene from the past, but not all ghosts are human, some are inanimate objects, feelings or sounds. There are enough documents, these testimonies in history, to prove this; and these documents refute the belief that ghosts are disembodied spirits.

Phantasms of the living" published in 1886, in two volumes, by the "Society for Psychical ressearch" of London is a good collection of paranormal stories and ghosts, which proves it.

For example, in one of these stories, an English officer and his family complain that a fine stagecoach regularly enters their yard. The stagecoach looked very real, and in one of his appearances, the officer's son headed for the car, in which a female form was evident, but the car disappeared before the boy could examine it properly; on the ground, there was no trace of a wheel or horseshoe.

Another valuable documentation, attesting to these paranormal facts, are the reports of UCLA anthropologist W.Y. Evans-Wentz. This magnificent book is a collection of stories, anecdotes and legends from the six regions where Celtic customs have persisted in the modern world. In 1907, the American anthropologist planned a two-year series of trips to Ireland, Scotland, Wales, Cornwall and England. The purpose of these trips was to report with people who claimed to have seen fairies or to have witnessed paranormal phenomena; for Evans-Wentz had noticed that the values of the twentieth century were gradually replacing the old beliefs. In one of these reports an old man living on the Isle of Man remarked to him this fact, with these words:

"Before education arrived on the island, there were many people who saw fairies, but now these witnesses are rare".

Education undoubtedly anathematizes the belief in paranormal phenomena and changes the way people approach life, causing an atrophy of their ability to see the past.

Evans-Wentz thus undertakes his journey from village to village, after having discussed with the witnesses of these paranormal phenomena which will be for the majority of the elderly and integrity, He quickly realized that these ghosts and fairies were not at all consistent with those represented in the collective imagination. The vast majority looked like normal people except they were as if lit from within and transparent.
These ghosts wore clothes of yesteryear and engaged in occupations of yesteryear, some hunted, others entered and emerged from the ruins of an old castle, others rang the bells of a ruined church; but what these ghosts seemed to appreciate the most was to make war with each other. A large number of witnesses claim to have seen medieval armies fighting, gathered in meadows or marshes, illuminated by the moon.

The places where these spectra of the past are most often isolated places, such as the middle of a forest, cemeteries, along a little frequented lake, or places with a busy historical past such as archaeological sites, the ruins of a medieval castle or an old battlefield. We are here in places that partially escape the three-dimensional physical world of humans, but we cannot yet speak of the fifth dimension. It is an intermediate level of integration into the fifth dimension that can be defined as the fourth dimension and the spirit of nature.

It is essential to emphasize the importance of the Moon in these visions, because these ghosts of the past are mostly either illuminated by the Moon, spotted with moonlight or illuminated from the inside by a light similar to that of the Moon.

I.4. THE DESERT OF THE REAL.

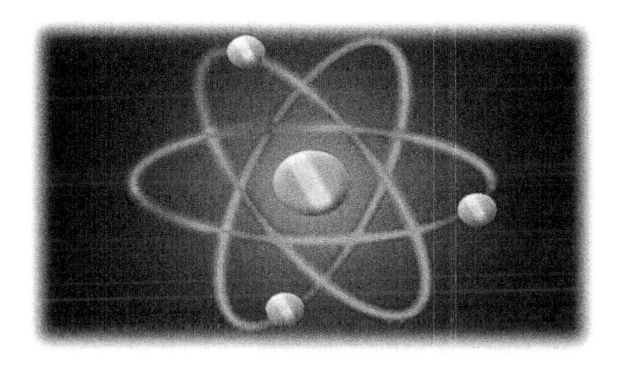

How to talk about "real" without mentioning the smallest thing that makes us up "the atom". We are not going to develop the atom in all its aspects, that would be a colossal job. However, the atom has very interesting characteristics that even the intellectual elite of our world still fail to discern. Yes, we are indeed talking about quantum physics, of the observation of the atom, and its strange behavior, which forces us to question the true nature of what we call "the real"

Everything is made up of atoms, and in everyday life, the average citizen has no idea to ask themselves, for example, when they come across an object, if it is present or not. There is no doubt thereon, when an observer sees an object it is right there. So why below one certain scale of measurement this reality is no longer there.

To understand this phenomenon, let us briefly talk about the world of atoms and particles, and imagine that a quantum particle accepts two possible states. To
simplify this example as much as possible, let's name these states "1" and "0", such as a switch. While the switch can only be in one state
at the same time, either "on" or "off", the particle itself found in what is called a superimposition of states, this means that simultaneously 1 and 0; and this superimposition of states disappears only when an observer decides to measure its state, causing a collapse of the wave function.
This first experience contradicts the possibility of a unique and objective reality for our quantum particle, its state therefore depends on the observer. The second anomaly is observed when we want to measure these quantum particles. There are many experiments that we call "delayed choice", which presents the anomaly as follows:

A quantum particle appears as two forms, either in a spread waveform in space, or in the form of a corpuscle which is point-like in space. According to experimental device used, the particle will adopt one or the other form.

So far, there are nothing abnormal, the anomaly is observed in the "delayed-choice experiments" in which there are has two measurement points. If we modify in progress of experiments, the measurement conditions at second point, it modifies the conditions of measurement of the first point, even if the particle has whether already crossed the first point. Which means the particle has crossed the first device of measurement either in the form of a wave or in the form of corpuscle, and that we change the measure to the level of the second point, this retroacts on the behavior of the particle since the beginning of the measure. Here we can see that information goes back in time.

These two examples reinforce the idea that we are constantly in an ocean of information and that it is "us", as observers, who interpret this information. It is our consciousness that therefore determines our "reality", and even the notion of "time" does not escape this reasoning. The real in the absence of an observer is equivalent to a desert.

I.5. DENSITY AND DIMENSION.

Our consciousness determines our reality, rather the state of our consciousness, and more precisely the energetic frequency of it.

Our reality can also be located. Compared to the level of our energy frequency, we will be located in one of the levels of space-time or outside of this one.

You have all heard of 2D, 3D,5D... The meaning of the D varies depending if the "D" means "Density" or "Dimensions".

But these two concepts are related, since it is our energy density, which determines, the dimension in which our consciousness is located.

When D = Density

The higher the energetic frequency of an entity will be high, the less dense it will be low, and vice versa, the more an entity's energy frequency will be low the more it will be dense.

The 1 D therefore corresponds to all kinds of entities or objects with a very low energetic oscillation.

For example: crystals, minerals, stones.

The 2D corresponds to entities with a higher energetic oscillation than those of the first density, but this energy is not still very high.
For example: The animal kingdom.

The 3D corresponds to the energetic frequency of most humans, the vast majority of whom will never manage to rise above this frequency. Since they can't go beyond the information collected by their meaning, these people are doomed to live in a material world.

The 4 D corresponds to the energetic frequency of the nature of the spirit, it is a intermediate frequency between 3 and 5, which can be experienced by doing a work of meditation, or sometimes in an innocuous way. The paranormal stories are good examples of this intermediate state.

The 5 D is the frequency of the extraterrestrials, it corresponds at all experiences made outside our space-time. For example: The astral projection, the near-death experiences, the dream...

The 6D is the end of the physical world.

When D = Dimension

Here, we are talking about the different dimensions of "the consciousness". Dimensions are states of consciousness accessible to each of us. provided that we vibrate at the frequency corresponding to the dimension, each dimension having a specific vibrational frequency, they will all have their own sets of specificities and of opportunities.

The 1D corresponds to the point of the source, the energetic point where it all began. This original energy that we all have within us. A metaphorical allusion is made to it in some religions, and esoteric doctrines, those here, teach their followers, that part of the divine (of God) dwells within each being.

The 2D is the dimension of duality, of good and evil, the feminine and the masculine, it is an emotional dimension.

The 3D is de dimension imposed on us since our day of birth, it is that of the physical world, the material world, individualism. The majority of humans are still at this level, however a slow but wide-ranging awakening is noticed and this is no coincidence.

The 4D is the dimension of integration, like the 4th density, the 4th dimension is an intermediate dimension. It is when a being begins to become aware that everything around him is not only physical and material. It's a dimension of permanent questioning. It is a quest for knowledge to achieve wisdom. The 4D acts as a purifying filter before the dimensions of excellence.

The 5D is the dimension of transcendence, of excellence and wisdom. The awareness of the individual of 5D greatly surpasses that of the average group. The 5th dimension is even lighter in frequency than the 4th, it is made of pure love, the consciousness of a being of 5D is cosmic and its reality is multidimensional.

The 6D is the dimension of co-creation. The individual is one with the matter that makes up its environment, he can act on it and even transform it.

It is important to note that the energetic frequency and the original and current dimension of our Universe is the 5D. We, as well as our planet, we are all held in this 3D fictional reality, but the wind has turned, every day of new consciousness awakens, the ascension of
Humanity towards 5D have begun.

This change, is also announced to us by the passage of Humanity to the Age of Aquarius. Age characterized by progress, technology, scientific thought, critical reason and freedom.

For some, we should wait for the year 3573, others fix this passage in the year 2160, for still others like the "New age" thinkers, the passage would be imminent. A lot of dates are proposed, for my part, I think that this event will happen between 2050 and 2080.

I.6. THE PLANETARY ENERGY NETWORK AND INTERDIMENSIONAL PORTALS.

To understand the "energies" and "energy portals," a reminder about the energy's operating mode is required. The universe is an ocean of frequencies; these frequencies are energies that interfere with each other. On Earth, it is gravity that propagates and condenses this flow of energy to where the physical object is formed. It is this interaction between these two frequencies that transforms this energy into matter. We also recall the role of the observer in this process, because it is the vibrational density of his consciousness that will determine the form of the matter. That is, the matter is visible only when it is subject to the interpretation of an observer. The observer who has knowledge of his own existence, creates time, and animates this potential energy, giving it values and meaning.

Since the big majority of humans vibrate in 3D, this interaction of energy will be translated, during its observation, in physical matter, while for beings of 5D or more, this interaction of energy will be interpreted as a place where two energies intersect in the universe.

All places in the material world, for example, like a place on our Earth, on the Moon of or Mars. All that places are scattered in this ocean of energy, which is itself influenced by the gravitational flow of certain energy values that are constantly evolving.

We call these locations "the physical places" that we can located in our space-time. Every place has energy knot that some call "chakras" and others call "energy centers." There are great energy centers in the world. For example, the Giza plateau is one of them. The three pyramids on the board are aligned with the three stars of the Orion's belt, and their greatness is proportional to the luminous intensity of the stars to which they relate.

The meridian of Giza separates the landmasses of our planet into two equal surfaces. that makes the great pyramid, the gravity center of the planet.

The Sphinx, which is basically a lion whose head was reworked, look eastward Nowadays, through to advances in astronomy, we can deduce that the builders of this monument had an increased knowledge of astronomy because the lion fixed the constellation of the same name, which rose exactly due east of Giza; there are 10500 years, which also gives us clues about the age of the Sphinx.

The coincidences continue with the height of the great pyramid; this one multiplied by a billion gives us the distance between the Earth and the Sun in meters. Our galaxy, the Milky Way, was a kind of celestial Nile for the ancient Egyptians. This is why a correlation is observable between the positioning of the three pyramids in relation to the Nile River, which is a representation of our Galaxy in Earth.

Why did the builders of these buildings work so painstakingly? Why this attention to detail? only to incarcerate unfortunate burial chambers of a few square meters in their breasts? Or should we rather consider the possibility that this complex had another function? In any case, all the clues point in this direction, and this complex could have been used to produce energy to power an energy portal to another dimension. This hypothesis seems less crazy when we analyze the energy and function of the planetary energy network.

The Earth is traversed by a set of fluxes of energy organized in several grids that are layered and interconnected. Imagine an energy mesh system that envelops and crosses our planet. This interconnected mesh system was discovered thanks to anomalies such as magnetic anomalies, geophysics, dowsing, and apparitions of UFOs. The energy nodes of this network have particular characteristics; perhaps for this reason, the old civilizations actually had centers for religion, philosophy, and the arts. What immediately catches the eye is the alignment of these sacred sites. They are not randomly built but rather on lines of precise geometries that correspond to the Earth's energy flow lines.

The Romans had discovered these lines; their columnists report that they have found straight lines drawn on the ground, or menhirs aligned, in almost all the conquered countries, in Europe, in Crete, in the region of Babylon, and in North Africa. These lines existed long before them, and I don't think the Romans didn't know the function of these energy lines, for most of their temples were built on them.

This geometric alignment of sacred sites is observable across all the planet, following are a few examples:

In England, we can observe the "ley" lines discovered in 1920 by Alfred Watkins, a photographer and British essayist, who theorized the phenomenon of site alignment in 1922 in his book "Early British Trackways".
The "ley lines" are either natural sites or ones built by human hands that are connected to each other in straight lines across Britain. These places are either linked to water (ponds, springs, sinks); either tumuli, dolmens, menhirs, stone circles, castles, churches, or particular hills.

In Germany, in 1929, Wilhelm Teudt, A German priest publishes a book entitled "Germanische Heiligtümer" (Germanic Sanctuaries), in which he reports the existence of sacred lines in central Germany. These lines connect ancient sites over hundreds of kilometers in a straight line and form geometric figures.

From Europe to Asia, an axis of 4000 km:

In 1950, the French writer Jean Richer, who is living in Greece, is researching Greek temples. He begins his investigation following a dream that can be described as premonitory because it claims that Apollo himself would have guided him. Be that as it may, the writer, once awake, will have the reflex of taking a map and drawing a line from the sanctuary of Apollo at Delphi towards the Acropolis of Athens. He then finds that this line can be extended to the island of Delos, which is the birthplace of Apollo, and to the temple of Apollo at Kamiros on the island of Rhodes.

His brother, Lucien Richer, continues the investigation and extends the line drawn by his brother towards the north-west and south-east, where he finds a lot of other correspondence dedicated this time to Saint-Michael.
The line crosses Greece, Italy, France, Great Britain, and Ireland. The northwest end is the sacred island of Skellig Michael in Ireland, and the south-east end will be Mount Carmel in Israel. There, the line splits to go to join sites in Egypt and Mecca. The Richer brothers come to connect an impressive number of religious sites on an axis of 4000 km called the axis St. Michael/Apollo.

We can also see the existence of a global line. This connects Easter Island, the Nazca geoglyphs, the fortress of Ollantaytambo, the pyramids of Paratoari, the rock museum of Tassili N'Ajjer in Algeria and the Giza pyramid. Giza is also aligned with Teotihuacan and the Chinese pyramid of Shen-His.

The elder civilizations had a knowledge and science that we forgot. How is it that such important knowledge has been subtracted from the global collective consciousness?
We live in the information age, yet humans have never been so stupid.
I will not go into the details of the "energies," like those of the Hartmann network, underground waterways, radon, those emanating from a fault, or those from a deposit of ore. Although these would be very exciting to develop, they would distract us from the subject. I therefore close this great parenthesis on the planetary energy grid that has allowed us to understand that we are constantly traversed by this flow of energy, that ancient civilizations were perfectly attuned to this fact, and that they even left us physical traces.

So, there are places on Earth where energies intersect and give rise to phenomena that official science, still, cannot explain to us.

Technically, we can try to explain these phenomena as well. When flows of energies of small volume intersect with a slow flow, this interaction can create a kind of energy bubble, that would be similar to small doors from which we could see, perceive or feel beings, objects, sensation or feeling from other dimensions, other universes, for a short time. These little winks of the eye are also called "the impressions of déjà vu".

These small gates of interdimensional energies are also the basis of all ghost stories, spirits, and jinns stories.

On the other hand, when high-volume, fast-flowing energy flows intersect, we have the possibility of being confronted with a large interdimensional vortex or portal.

Here we are talking about natural and physical portals, not sentimental portals.

A natural energy portal comes in the shape of an energy bubble or a tridimensional round space. One of the characteristics that present the large portals, that is, portals large enough to envelop a person or a group of people, is the systematic presence of fog. Once in contact with this portal, you feel a sense of lightness, as if an invisible energy were carrying you, which is not wrong because you are literally routed to places present in other dimensions. Portals work both ways and can also be entered unintentionally.

History is full of such stories, but even in this case, people or objects having entered the portal do not find themselves projected into the void of space because the portals maintain similar harmonics, that is, energy and math factors are similar, and this harmony between the portals is essential and necessary. This also explains why the portal is shared between the two places. The object, once it has passed the portal, is sent to a similar place, i.e., a place with similar harmonics; it could be any place compatible with these frequencies. For example, the person could be on Earth now but on another planet in another time, and it will happen as long as there is frequency correspondence between these two portals.

There are still ancient artificial portals active on Earth. The Bermuda triangle portal is one of them. This area located within a triangle formed by the Bermuda archipelago, Miami in Florida and San Juan in Puerto Rico, is a very important global energy center. Our friends of the federation let us know, that there are in the depths of the ocean, pyramidal structures dating from the era of the Atlanteans, similar to those of Giza, but unlike the pyramids of Giza those of Bermuda are still active. These are very old artificial portals that concentrate the scattered energy at a single point to create an interdimensional portal.

There are disappearances of military aircraft as civilians, some disappeared while they were receiving the final landing instructions from the control tower. Some fought against this zone of hyper turbulence for hours and once out of it, they noticed that barely a minute had passed.
There are also a large number of boat disappearances in Bermuda, some will be found later without their crew, others will be found years later with their goods intact, but no sign of the bodies of the crew or passengers.

For example, the disappearance of the SS Marine Sulphur Queen in 1963 is one of the most mysterious in modern merchant navy history. This 154-metre oil tanker converted to transport liquid sulphur disappeared at sea and was never found. The investigation could not clearly explain what had happened. On 04 February 1963, at 01:25, the crew sent a routine message indicating its position: the cargo ship was located at coordinates 25°45' N, 86°W, that is to say near the islands of southern Florida. This message will be the last of the ship that will disappear with its 39 crew members.

There are so many cases of mysterious disappearance recorded in this region that we are spoiled for choice for examples.

In March 1918, a huge American Navy coal miner, the USS Cyclops, suddenly and mysteriously disappeared on a trip between the West Indies and Baltimore. Even today, we wonder how such a large ship could disappear without a trace.

The USS Cyclops was a ship belonging to the fleet of the American Navy, a ship that measured nearly 153 meters, with a crew of 306 people. Since its commissioning in 1910, the ship has sailed mainly between the Baltic Sea, the Caribbean and Mexico and was used to transport coal around the world.

In 1948, a Douglas DC-3 aircraft flying between Puerto Rico and Florida mysteriously disappeared, and its last message was, "We are approaching the airport… We are now only 80 km south… We see the lights of Miami… All is well. Wait for the instructions for the landing."

Since the beginning of the 19th century, mysterious disappearances have been recorded in this area, on average, there are 4 planes and 20 boats that mysteriously disappear each year. The last disappearance was recorded in December 2020. A boat with 20 people disappears between the Bimini islands of the Bahamas and Florida, the search has not yielded anything.

The Bermuda triangle is the best known of the areas with disconcerting characteristics, but there are still 11 around the world, which have the same characteristics as the triangle of the devil, that is to say magnetic anomalies, energy aberrations, time distortions, disappearances of boats and planes and other strange phenomena such as compass, radio and control panels breakdowns.

These 11 anomaly zones are the South Pole, the North Pole, the Dragon Triangle also called the Devil's Sea near Japan, in Hawaii the Hamakulia volcano region, near Easter Island, the loyalty islands in New Caledonia, the Wharton basin in Australia, Great Zimbabwe, the Sahara Desert in Algeria, the megaliths of the Zingh Empire, the South Atlantic and Mohenjo-darro in Pakistan.

What is even more surprising is that these places are equidistant and arranged in a regular way around the globe.

These artificial portals are very old, they were swallowed up during what the whole planet knows as the flood. The biblical episode of the flood is an allegorical story that has many variations around the world, I detailed this subject in two of my books namely «Historia 2.0» and «The encyclopedia of extraterrestrial races», so I will not dwell any longer on the subject. What must nevertheless be remembered is the fact that the peoples of this World, now engulfed, were technologically ahead of us.

We can also find on Earth many modern artificial portals belonging to the members of this blue blood cabal and controlled by the military-industrial complex. They are located mainly in the «DUMBs» «Deep Underground Military Bases», to date more than 10,000 underground bases have been identified throughout the planet. Some of these bases are equipped with small or medium-sized portals, these portals are used by this cabal as part of the "SSP" program, "Secret Space Program". Since the federation's return in the wake of the Earth, they have been prohibited from leaving the planet. They are currently in quarantine. It is impossible for them to leave the Earth by propelled means, which is why they use the last portals in their possession.

The most used portal is that of the secret base of the Red Sea which is on an island 8 km from the Yemeni coast.

We also have the one of zone51 which is used regularly, its entrance is at the exit of Los Angeles, near the bay of Santa Monica.

CERN in Switzerland is also one of these artificial portals belonging to these toxic races. It would be very naive of us to think that these entities with a slave mentality would suddenly change their behavior to start working for the good of Humanity. They would never have invested in such an expensive project without having an interest in return. Here, billions were spent to create this artificial portal under a completely phony cover, which was to get the "particle of God". Our greedy and selfish capitalists would have suddenly become patrons. CERN is built exactly on Ley's lines. It is a retro-engineering project aiming to create a giant portal. There are also portals of immeasurable size in space, they are detected by very sensitive energy sensors and used by the ships of the galactic federation. These giant portals are either fixed so their locations are known and listed, or small, in this case they are difficult to detect, because they appear and disappear almost randomly and never in the same places.

II. MY EXPERIENCES.

"I'm dead and I don't find it creepy. I feel like I'm in "another dimension". I know it may sound crazy but I find myself in a white, soft, beautiful and bright space that has no limit. I am in a state of love and feeling extremely powerful. I feel good."

Fabienne Raoul. Testimony on her NDE.

II.1. MY NEAR-DEATH EXPERIENCES.

I had the chance to experience this phenomenon twice. I only partially remember the details of my first NDE but my second experience was very disturbing, even magical

I was 27 when I had this serious accident where I lost a lot of blood. I was driven by one of my colleagues to the emergency room of a hospital where doctors and nurses were slow to take charge of me. I was standing at the entrance, in front of a medical secretary, who was asking me lots of questions, while my two hands, which I had clumsily wrapped in two t-shirts, presented severe cuts, very deep.
The blood no longer spat, but the T-shirts turned red-blood could no longer absorb my blood which began to flow on the ground.

I could hardly say a few words that were "I think I'll faint". It was only after these words that the staff activated, finally, and took charge of me. I was always awake on a bed, in an emergency room of the hospital, the doctor, after questioning me in turn, offered to sew my wounds without anesthesia, for him my condition was stable, I was alert and showed no signs of weakening. I could not look at this big needle that pierced my flesh several times, but something strange was beginning to happen, something I felt for the first time. One thing, like a little bubble of air coming up from my left foot to my heart, it was not painful but a strange sensation invaded me, the bubble arrived at the level of my heart, I turned to the doctor to say " I think this is the end for me!" , he did not have time to reply that this little bubble, at the level of my heart turned into an intense pinch, but of very short duration. I can describe the pain of this pinch, like a small needle. And there... nothing more, except the absolute black, I wondered, for a moment, if I had died, but at the same time, I was still there, in any case a part of me remained; no doubt what the scholars called the spirit, the soul or the conscience. No angel of death, no Grim reaper. I had a little pain for my family that I was leaving behind, but at the same time, I could not do anything for them. A feeling of comfort filled me afterwards. I felt like an energy, I floated, relieved to be released from this fleshly envelope. So that was death! I was waiting for the

next stage, and suddenly I had a vision, I was on the side of a mountain of black rock, I saw in the distance similar mountains surrounding a lake of reddish color, it was night, only lightning illuminated from time to time the place. I stood there for a moment observing the surroundings, wondering if this was «the other world», if this was where I was going to remain the rest of my existence, when two indescribable creatures pretended to attack me twice, these entities opened their mouths towards my direction and entrenched themselves on the side of the mountain, it seemed to amuse them. I quickly left this place and found myself in the shape of energy.
I floated, a feeling of power and intense love enveloped me, until I was like reaspired in my body. I woke up in hyperventilation, a while was necessary for me to return to my normal state. The doctor then told me that my brain had not been oxygenated for several seconds, I replied that I had visions of horror; but when the doctor asked me again about my visions, I could not answer him, It was as if I had forgotten everything, as if someone had suddenly pressed the "Delete" key on my brain. I was able to more or less reconstruct the silhouette of these beings from other worlds, after several years, thanks to testimonies, in a documentary, of people who had experienced the NDE. Some of these people had seen similar entities and unlike me, they remembered them. They were humanoid types with reptile faces. This

is the best description, but remains a description, because these entities do not exist in our world, we can only try to describe them with codes and images known by all. The strangest feeling after being revived was this feeling of imprisonment, I was sad, because I felt limited again, when I should have been very happy not to have died.

II.2. EXTRATERRESTRIAL PHENOMENA.

Brussels, 29 November 1989, a few weeks after the fall of the Berlin Wall. This period, beginning in late 1989 and ending around the summer of 1991, will enter the literature as "the Belgian wave of UFOs". I was seven years old, and I slept on a bunk bed, on the back floor of our two-storey house, with my older brother. Our room had a very large attic window overlooking a large garden.

I often observed the reflection of the moon light on the wall facing the large window before falling asleep, and strangely, that night, we had not one, but two luminous reflections on the wall.

The first was positioned on the right end of the wall while the second on the left end. Surprised and with the naivety of a seven-year-old child, I warned my big brother, "Oh, it's weird, this night we have two moons!". My brother paid no attention to it, retorting that I should try to sleep. But as I insisted, he finally gave in to my whims and rose to observe the anomaly. And there, no luck for him, the two white luminous balls to which a third was added, changed place. We observed three moons rotating on our wall. It looked like a propulsion engine consisting of three giant headlights rotating around a central axis. We used to see this kind of engine on American movie spaceships. My brother, impressed, fell on his butt. After this anomaly, we rushed to the window, but the flying object had disappeared.

The next day, the country was shaken. The media only talked about this phenomenon, SOBEPS, the Belgian society of space phenomena, had collected 143 testimonies. The UFO had been observed in Brussels, but especially in the border region with Germany, Verviers and Eupen. Apparently other people had been luckier than us, they were able to observe the object very closely.
Here are their testimonies:

Two gendarmes (Nicollet von Montigny) patrolling that night in the heights of Eupen, testify to the anomaly:

We saw big headlights under a craft that we did not know how to define, and I must tell you that the ground was really lit. It could have read the gazette. I saw a triangle, three headlights and an orange flashing ball. While we were watching this one, suddenly from behind the trees arose the other craft. Same power of lighting with a rapidity, as if it had been catapulted. Everyone listened to our post. Some laughed. They thought of Saint Nicholas. They were scared like us.

Dieter Plumans, a retired constable at "La Calamine", says:

- If I remember correctly, we had already seen something. The patrol from Calamine had taken the road to Henri-Chapelle then stopped at the foot of a motionless and silent UFO, just above a rest house. The two gendarmes kept their composure for a few minutes, then the UFO disappeared in the sky.

Here is one of the 143 testimonies, collected by SOBEPS:

"Let's say it was huge and it was shaped like a triangle." I went to the window to see and I saw all these little lights, like stars.

After these testimonies, the president of SOBEPS concluded:

"- They are not laser beams, let alone holograms. It is clearly a material and solid object that has moved through space. '

Steven Spielberg's E.T. movie was very popular, and we were living our own alien story. After that day everything became possible. For almost three years, more than 200 observations will be made in Belgium. We felt we were at the advent of an incredible thing, which had to happen, given the frequency of UFO sightings in the Belgian sky, it had to happen, but nothing happened, nothing happens because what we were seeing was the ASTRA TR3b or XRZ aircraft. A plane with magnetohydrodynamic propulsion, triangular shape. The triangular machine with futuristic curves used the magnetic force of the Earth, was surprisingly silent and could move to more than Mac10, no more and no less than a prototype of the American army. Unfortunately, there was nothing extraterrestrial, but human technology well ahead of its time. It is for this reason that the Belgian UFO wave cannot be considered as a decisive proof of the existence of extraterrestrials, but on the other hand, it is a very good example proving that a UFO should not be automatically assimilated to «extraterrestrial», although it is highly likely that during those two years, some of them were obviously.

*

I have always been fond of celestial observation. From an early age, I looked at the sky, this observation made during the Belgian wave of UFOs in 1989 has certainly permanently marked my unconscious, but apart from that, I think I simply maintained a peculiarity present in the human DNA, while many we neglected to do so.

For more than 15 years, I have been observing the sky almost every night with good quality equipment. I remain an amateur astronomer, but I have improved a lot in this discipline, I can now recognize the different constellations, star clusters, nebulae and galaxies, name and locate the brightest planets and stars in the sky.

I know the difference between a shooting star, a meteorite or a satellite, and I can persuade you, that every other day, I observe strange lights that have nothing to do with the celestial objects I just listed above. For example, almost every night, I observe one or more white lights, these are shaped like small white spheres and roam the sky at full speed.
When the trajectory, of these luminous balls, is stable and their speed constant, the astronomers attribute this phenomenon to the movements of the satellites,

then these satellites are observable almost every night and this is not a paranormal phenomenon, only when these white balls accelerate their course and change course abruptly, we can no longer speak of displacement of satellites, we are then at the heart of a paranormal phenomenon and this kind of movement of objects is observable every other day or on three.

The last time I watched these white balls, they behaved very strangely. I followed with my astronomical binoculars one of these white balls, which as every night crossed the sky at high speed, visibly "another satellite" and the moment I prepared to observe another part of the sky, suddenly the white light met a similar light. The two luminous balls went around and took opposite trajectories at a blazing speed and then disappeared.

Finally, on the night of July 23, 2022, I was able to observe, with two members of my family who are generally skeptical about the subject of aliens, a very strange phenomenon.

We were in Antalya, Turkey on the balcony of our hotel room overlooking the Mediterranean Sea, the sky was clear and it had just been dark.

I was watching the sky, a white light caught my attention, I watched it for a moment with my binoculars, the light was static,

but very bright and did not correspond to any of
the stars or planets I used to observe in this part of
the sky. After a few minutes of observation, seeing
that the light was not moving, I began to observe
the other parts of the sky, when suddenly the light
moved. I immediately zoomed on the object with
my binoculars and whispered at the same time "
you my friend, you are not a planet!". It was
probably these words that alerted the other two
members of my family who asked me more details
about this strange light and then begged me to lend
them my binoculars that I was against heart,
because the object resembled a large luminous
sphere circumvented by moving rings of the same
color, imagine the planet Saturn moving towards
you at full speed. The light moved in our direction
and disappeared in a cloud of light that had just
opened before it. The cloud of light disappeared in
turn. The members of my family remained
speechless on this balcony facing this strange
phenomenon that we had just experienced, they
are now less skeptical about the UFO phenomenon,
As for me, I had the impression in the depths of me
to have been warmly greeted by these beings from
beyond the world that I greeted in return.

II.3. STRANGE DREAMS.

I had the chance to experience several kinds of dreams that I would like to share with you. Two of them were very special.

I had the chance to experience lucid dreaming. Often the dreamer is not aware of the fact that he is dreaming, except in the case of a lucid dream. There are all kinds of techniques for experiencing this, rather than knowing that you are dreaming, such as counting your fingers, controlling a specific detail of your body such as a tattoo or a text that you would have previously written on a part of your body… But everything plays out once again in your brain, the brain has to click and once this click is realized everything becomes possible.

In my case, I didn't use any of these little tricks. I simply lay down with the will to have a lucid dream and after a few weeks this happens. I was standing in my living room and I quickly understood that it was a dream without controlling other parameters. After a little mischievous smile, I thought if it was a dream, I could do anything. I hurried to experience the flight. Afraid to be awake at any moment. So, I started floating in my living room several meters from the ground. The next step was to cross the wall that led me to my garden, which I did without difficulty. I was planning to fly to distant counties that suddenly I woke up. This dream was too short, but the feeling was majestic.

Dream within a Dream.

I remember a really banal dream, in which I was in a car parked along a green space, a group of young people looked at me and one of them smiled at me. I then wake up in my living room, on my sofa bed, I go to the kitchen to prepare a meal, I prepare a TV tray, I sit in front of my TV and suddenly I find myself again waking up on my sofa bed. The TV set I hadn't started was gone.
So, I woke up a second time, this time for good? I then go back to the kitchen to prepare my meal. For a few minutes, I wondered, if I was going to wake up again, if I was stuck in a time loop.

The rest of the day, the interactions I had with family members and friends or other people seemed artificial to me. I had dreamed in my dream and was still waiting to be awakened, I really felt like I had experienced several parallel dimensions and was stuck in one of them. I challenge scientists to find a rational explanation for this experience that was for me more real than reality. Here is what I call a wink of the matrix.

III. PARANORMAL COMPENDIUM.

"There is a chance in billions that our reality is right, the universe is a simulation created by a superintelligence."

Elon Musk.

III.1. DIVINE PUNISHMENT.

The Facts:

Liverpool, Casablanca or Amsterdam, this story has many variations and has toured the world several times via social networks.

In reality, we do not know exactly where this story takes place and anyway it does not matter, since it has no basis. The story tells us about a dispute between a mother and her daughter. The mother is reading the Holy Quran, in the adjacent room, her daughter listens to rock music.

The volume of the music is so high that the mother is disturbed and asks her daughter several times to decrease the volume. The third attempt of the mother will be the last, because the teenager, tired by the requests of her mother, will tear the Koran from her hands to tear the pages. The divine punishment will be almost immediate, the girl will be transformed into a creature resembling a fusion between a human and a rat or a human and a macaque, it again depends on the versions.

The teenager will then be hospitalized, unwanted by her parents and irretrievable physically, the girl will finally be euthanized.

It is also during her stay at the hospital that she will be photographed and her story will be known by the general public.

Analysis:

As mentioned earlier, there is nothing paranormal in this story that was probably invented from scratch. The alleged photo of the girl, used in social media, is actually a wax statue made by Australian sculptor Patricia Piccinini.

It was exhibited in 2003 in a museum in the Netherlands.

Therefore, the claim that the photo was taken in the hospital is false, there is no girl transformed into a creature, nor family demanding her death.

The story is false on the other hand the gains generated through it, they are very real. Some have found the way to make money by exploiting fear and especially ignorance of the masses.

III.2. THE CRIES OF DAMNED SOULS.

This audio recording, containing terrifying human moans and screams, went around the world via social networks and was very popular in religious circles.

The Facts:

The source of this anecdote is more than doubtful. The tape was recorded in Siberia by a team of Russian scientists led by Doctor Azzacov during an oil well drilling.
The team reportedly drilled a 14.9 km deep hole and fell on a cavity.
Intrigued by this discovery, the scientists decided to place a microphone and other sensory analysis instruments. The microphone recorded human screams and screams at a depth of 14.9 km under a heat of more than 1100 degrees Celsius.

After this discovery, the frightened team stopped the study. Later, the story spread throughout the world, first by word of mouth, then through social networks, essentially religious.

The 38-second recording, approved by several members of the Christian clergy, will be launched as the discovery "of the tormented cries of the damned souls". So, our scientists would have drilled a hole leading directly to purgatory. This story will later have multiple versions, in one of them, Dr Azzacov would be a convinced atheist who would have said:

"After this discovery, I believe in the existence of hell".

The soundtrack was analyzed by several sound engineers and the content of this anecdote by truth seekers. The result is unequivocal. The truth seekers found no trace of the existence of the Russian geologist Azzocov or the alleged scientists who accompanied him during his study.

The results of the analyses made by the sound engineers, on the audio recording in question, are unequivocal, for example for Osman Can Okkasöz, special effects specialist and sound engineer who has to his credit many films and documentaries, The soundtrack is definitely fake.

Okkasöz analysis:

"There is no doubt that this sound mix you hear is very impressive at first. His goal is to scare the listeners as much as possible and he obviously succeeds. If such a recording would have circulated, 15-20 years ago, that is, before digital sound recording technology developed, many people would have taken this as a paranormal phenomenon, because it was much more difficult to produce such a sound mix in analog recording systems. But now, in 2020, we get amazing mixes on the digital tables that we use to edit the sound recordings of the movies and we are even able to turn these sounds for example into the sound of fans of a football stadium with thousands of people. In this respect, although the recording we are listening to had a really scary structure, it is still possible to produce a similar one in studio conditions. You can borrow sounds from some horror movies and spend an hour or two at the recording table to easily prepare a collage that gives the same effect.

We can therefore conclude that the cries of the damned souls did not come from purgatory, but from a mixer. This anecdote is to be classified among the successful hoaxes of the internet.

III.3. THE MUMMY OF RAMESSES II. THE CURSED PHARAOH.

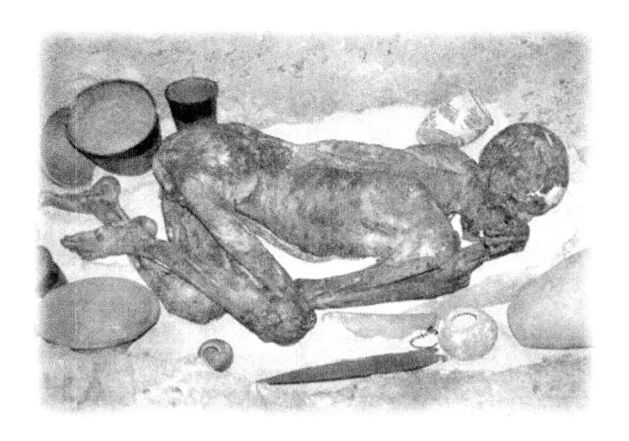

The Facts:

Late 1980s, early 1990s, no internet or social networks. The photo of the mummified and deteriorated body of this poor Egyptian villager, encoded as EA32751 at the British Museum in London, is making headlines. Again, some religious circles, mainly Muslims, exaggerate the importance of this mummy, which scientifically and historically has nothing to do with Pharaoh Ramses II.

Muslim religious circles exploit this photo and seek to create a small miracle by correlating it with certain passages of the Holy Quran. Specifically, Verses 90, 91 and 92 of Sura Jonah. Which could be translated into French as follows:

90. And We sent the Children of Israel across the sea. Pharaoh and his armies pursued them with determination and enmity. Then when the drowning had reached him, he said, "I believe there is no other divinity but the One who believed the children of Israel. And I am one of the submitters."
91. Is it now that you are subject? Whereas before you disobeyed. And that you were among the corrupters.
92. Today we will spare your body, so that you may become a sign to your successors. Yet many people pay no attention to Our (warning) signs.

So, this body, which for years was exhibited at the British Museum, would have been that of Ramses II. The body of the cursed Pharaoh who would suddenly resurface as a sign of divine warning.

Analysis:

Scientifically and historically, there is no probability that this object encoded with the identification number EA32751 at the British Museum in London, either the body of Ramses II, or that of another Pharaoh.

There are still about fifteen mummies of the same kind, inventoried at the British Museum in London. The mere fact of making the connection with Ramses II or another pharaoh makes the specialists smile.

Today, with advances in science and new technologies in the field of archaeology, the biblical episode of the exodus itself is historically contested.

In addition, the mummy of Ramses II was discovered in 1881 in the Valley of the Kings, its excavated body is currently on display in the Cairo Museum.

According to Derek A. Welsby, an Egyptologist and currently curator of antiquities at the British Museum in London, «scientifically and historically no connection is possible between the mummy exhibited at the British Museum and that of any pharaoh». The specialist claims that the fact that the mummy's body is half-damaged and its internal organs remain intact, is not a miracle in itself, because when a body, after its death, is quickly buried in the desert, the intense heat causes the water contained in its organs to evaporate quickly and the body fossilizes. In addition, a considerable amount of mummies of the same type have been found in many other desert regions of Egypt and in the Nazca plain of Peru. It is exhibited in various museums around the world. Welsby gives us other details about the body that completely destroy the possibility of the miracle. The body was found during an official search in the city of Gibeleyn in Upper Egypt, that is to say more than 300km from the Red Sea, this information geographically invalidates the possibility that this mummy is that of Ramses II. Moreover, during the same search, no particular jewel, clothing or sign was found in the tomb that would reveal the privileged identity of the corpse.

We know that the ancient Egyptians used to bury their relatives with the objects they used in their daily lives. These everyday objects and gold jewelry give us valuable information about the social rank of the deceased. The utensils that we can observe around the mummy of the British Museum are original objects of the tomb. These are terracotta materials, quite ordinary, used by ordinary people of that time. If this person is the "cursed pharaoh" mentioned in the sacred texts, then there is no reason for him to be in an ordinary ordained tomb, the interior and surroundings of which have been arranged and decorated by other people; it would make more sense to find it randomly in the vicinity of the Red Sea.

I sincerely believe that these false miracles strongly deteriorate the image of religions and that these pseudo-religious scholars should inform themselves, before making statements lacking intelligence.

III.4. THE LEGENDARY PHOTO OF THE DJINN.

supposed photo of the djinn.

The Facts:

A djinn is a supernatural creature of Arabian mythology. It is a creature with polarity most often negative, of a dimension parallel to ours. Djinns can be channeled by some humans and can show themselves in various forms, but under no circumstances materialize. Therefore, no physical interaction is possible with these beings. In the Holy Quran the djinn is described as being a creature conceived from a "smoke-free fire". I think that if I wanted to describe, to a predominantly uneducated population, the conception of a being appearing in the form of a hologram, I could not have found better words.

Precisely the source of this photo seems to be the young religious Internet users of the United Arab Emirates.

The young religious share and broadcast to the whole world a photo on which we can observe a strange being, this being strangely resembles a demon or a imp that could be observed in American films. Even the fact that some parts of the photo have been retouched does not hinder the dissemination of the picture of the djinn who meets a worldwide success. Young Internet users will even pretend that they had different experiences worthy of the greatest horror movies with the so-called djinn.

Analysis:

Although the dissemination of the photo on the internet seems to come from young religious Internet users in the United Arab Emirates, in reality the source of the photo is totally different. The photo comes from the Sommerset region in England, more precisely from one of the tourist caves of the village of Cheddar, whose most popular attraction of the site is the underground adventure circuit called "The Crystal Quest".

"The Crystal Quest" is a walk through the caves of the village of Cheddar inspired by the imaginary world of Tolkien. The caves are filled with reflective lakes and limestone sculptures depicting elves, demons or other imaginary creatures. The caves are illuminated like a fairy tale and mysterious songs emanating from hidden speakers, accompany visitors.

Our famous djinn is part of one of the many limestone sculptures that decorate the caves of the promenade "The Crystal Quest".

As for the photo, it was taken in 1995 by an English businessman named John X. who later invented this story from scratch. During his visit to the Cheddar caves, the businessman reportedly photographed models of elves and demons. After a while, John X. went to Saudi Arabia for a business trip, and gave, just to joke, a duplicate of the photo of the little Cheddar demon to a group of young Arabs he had met, telling them that he had photographed a djinn in England. The young Saudis immediately accepted the picture of the djinn, accompanied by his little story imagined from scratch by the English businessman, without questioning the slightest detail. Following this erroneous behavior of the young Saudis, the photo spread in waves from Saudi Arabia to all the countries of the Middle East in record time.

III.5. MARY TOFT, THE RABBIT WOMEN.

Is it possible that a woman is fertilized by an animal and that she gives life to about twenty rabbits? Or that she gives birth prematurely to parts of their bodies?

We are in 1726 in England, more precisely in Godalming in the Surey. Mary Toft, a 26 year old peasant girl, has a miscarriage. One of her neighbors who attended the scene notes that she gave birth of various animal members and decides to gather the pieces of flesh and show them to Ann Toft, Mary's mother-in-law, who is also a midwife.

It was she who decided to send the samples from her daughter-in-law to an experienced birth attendant in the town of Guildford named John Howard. Howard will see Mary who will show her other parts of animals from her effort last night. Howard, after examining Mary and her evidence, will find nothing conclusive. It was only when Mary reoffended, after a few days, that Howard decided to continue his investigation. Mary Toft will give birth with the help of John Howard, a few days apart, pieces of various animals such as cat legs, rabbit legs, rabbit bodies still in formation, but also about twenty rabbits often born dead and sometimes still alive. Stunned by these small miracles, John Howard decided to write to Henry Davenant, a member of the court of King George I. Davenant, after examining Toft and the evidence provided by Howard, will return to London convinced. The story grew when Davenant presented his conclusions to the royal family, who sent Nathanaël Saint-André, a Swiss surgeon at the king's court, to Guildford, and Samuel Molyneux, secretary to the Prince of Wales. In front of them, Toft will produce the torso of a rabbit that the royal surgeon will examine thoroughly. Nathanael Saint-André placed a piece of lung in the water and after seeing it floating, he deduced that the rabbit had indeed grown in the fallopian tubes of Toft. Toft produced the same evening in front of Saint-André and Molyneux a rabbit skin, followed by a cat head.

Very interested in this strange story, the King will send a second surgeon to have a second opinion. Cyriacus Ahlers royal surgeon will examine Toft and unlike his colleagues, he will find no trace of pregnancy in Mary, by cons the fact that the woman was in a state of constant tension and that she squeezed her thighs against each other as if to hold something inside her uterus did not escape her. Ahlers will return to London with the certainty that this story was a hoax and he will provide the evidence through the analyses made on the samples, animal parts, from Mary Toft, which he will obtain from Howard.

Cyriacus Ahlers will prove that these different animal parts were cut with sharp tools, he will also observe pieces of straw and cereals in the feces of the animals, which is obviously impossible to observe in newborns.

The doubt settled and they decided to take Toft back to London to examine him more closely.
The press got involved and the story became an urban legend. Within two months, Toft had become a celebrity.
Londoners jostled to see him, his portrait was painted, press articles were piling up and very few people were skeptical, while inside the hospital, the deception ended.

Mary Toft under surveillance could not produce any animal parts and after a few weeks, she confessed. Mary Toft, with the help of several accomplices, introduced the different pieces of animals into her vagina to then simulate her deliveries.

She explained to the judge that a traveler had taught her how to insert rabbits into her vagina and claimed that such a scheme would make her famous and rich. Mary Toft will be infamous and will not make a fortune. She will be incarcerated and will serve 5 months in prison for "cheating and abominable imposture by claiming to have given several monstrous births", this story will occupy England from the beginning of November 1726 until early January 1727.

III.6. THE PRESIDENT'S PREMONITORY DREAMS. ABRAHAM LINCOLN.

Abraham Lincoln (1809-1865) was the 16th president of the United States. Sadly known for having been assassinated in 1965 at the Ford Theatre in Washington D.C., the President gave much importance to dreams and their meaning. He often had premonitory dreams, which he shared with his relatives.

The herald ship of victory:

Lincoln was the President of the United States during the American Civil War, and before every major victory against the Confederates, he said he dreamed of a ship sailing at full speed. Before Johnston's surrender, he had the same dream, which he shared with General Ulysses S.Grant. That day, the President asked General Grant for news on the situation at the front. He replied that he was waiting for a letter that he should no longer delay and the following dialogue occurred between the two men:

Lincoln: - You will hear about it very quickly and the news will be important!

Grant: - Why do you think that?

Lincoln: - Because I had a dream last night; and since the beginning of the war, I have always had the same dream before every important military event! For example, at Bull Run, Antietam, Gettysburg! Turning to Welles, the secretary of the navy, he went on, this also concerns you, Mr. Welles. In the dream I had, I saw a ship sailing very quickly; and I'm sure it foreshadows an important national event!

This type of dream, mentioned by Abraham Lincoln, one among many, frequently occurred in his life, especially when he led the Northern Army. The President had learned to associate the dream of a ship sailing in the open sea, at high speed, with the imminent arrival of important news most often military victories.

The firearm:

Abraham Lincoln dreamed of his last son Thomas, nicknamed Tad, and hurriedly wrote to his wife Mary Todd:

"I think you better put away Tad's gun, I had a horrible dream about it"

One can deduce from these few lines, that despite her young age, Tad had a penchant for playing with firearms, that the President's wife had a very developed spiritual sense and that she gave much importance to her husband's premonitory dreams, because after reading this letter, Mary will take the necessary measures to avoid the worst for the little boy.

The death of a president:

Three days before his assassination, anxious Abraham Lincoln told his dream to his wife, his bodyguard, Ward Hill Lamon, and two other people in the room at the time. His bodyguard, Ward Hill Lamon, would have immediately transcribed the Speaker's dream and wrote:

Lincoln was shot and said that this strange dream had haunted and possessed him for several days. He said:

"About ten days ago I stayed up very late waiting for important dispatches from the front. Very soon after I went to bed, I fell asleep because I was exhausted. I started dreaming very quickly. Around me, there was a mortal calm. Then I heard choked sobs, as if several people were crying. I think I left my bed and walked around the lower floors. There, the silence was broken by the same heartbreaking tears, but the mourners remained invisible. I wandered from room to room; no living being was in sight, however when I passed, I encountered the same dismal sounds of distress. All the rooms were lit each object was familiar to me. But where were all these people who were crying like their hearts were breaking?

I was perplexed and alarmed. What could be the meaning of all this? Determined to find the cause of this state of affairs so mysterious and so shocking,
I continued until I reached the East Room into which I entered.
 There I met a disgusting surprise. Before me was a catafalque on which rested a corpse wrapped in funeral clothes. Around him were posted soldiers who behaved like guards. And there was a crowd of people among whom some looked sadly at the corpse whose face was covered, and others wept pitifully. Who died in the White House? -, I asked one of the soldiers. 'The president was his answer. 'He was murdered! – Then came a burst of grief from the crowd."

Lincoln tried to reassure his relatives about the meaning of his dream, telling them that the dream probably meant nothing, did he believe it himself? Because three days later, he was murdered by the Confederates. The President had indeed dreamed of his own death, but had not been able to predict his assassination.

III.7. CARL GUSTAV JUNG'S SYNCHRONICITIES

How to talk about synchronicity without mentioning the name of the greatest researcher in this field. Carl Gustav Jung (1875-1961) was a physician, professor, psychiatrist, psychotherapist, psychologist and essayist. He is undoubtedly one of the greatest thinkers of the 20th century. We owe to Jung the concept of "Synchronicity". Let us remember, a synchronicity is the simultaneous occurrence in the mind of an individual of at least two mental events that do not present a physical causal link, but whose association takes on a meaning for the person who perceives them. Synchronicities, the life of the Swiss psychotherapist abound here are some examples:

The explosion:

This story takes place in Vienna in the home of Sigmund Freud, of whom Jung was one of the first disciples and from whom he later separated due to theoretical and personal differences. The two men talk about parapsychology and their discussion is virulent. While Sigmund Freud found Carl Gustav Jung's ideas absurd and rejected them, Jung found that Freud was too materialistic and invited him to be more open-minded. Jung tells us the facts as follows:

While Freud was talking, something very strange happened to me. My chest hardened and became hot. At this very moment, the sound of a loud explosion came to us from the library that stood right beside us. The intensity of this sound was so strong that we were startled with fear. We were both standing and I looked at Freud and said, "This is what I call an example of a paranormal phenomenon!".
He replied that all these things were just nonsense. I was pissed and I said in turn: "No Professor, you are wrong! And to prove to you that I am right, I claim that a second explosion will take place! " As soon as I had finished speaking, a second explosion occurred, still emanating from the library.
I still wouldn't tell you what made me so confident at that moment.

Freud just looked at me with bulging eyes and we could not debate this phenomenon with him, neither that day nor another day.

The Golden Scarab:

The story of the golden scarab is surely the most famous story of synchronicity. Carl Gustav Jung is in consultation with one of his patients who was going through a period of severe depression. Between his multiple problems, his patient tells him about his dream of the day before. She mentions the fact that in her dream, a person offered her a golden scarab, and strangely enough, as soon as the patient mentions the name of the insect, it bumps against the window of Jung's office. The psychiatrist then opens the window, grabs the insect, turns to the woman and says "there it is! Your golden scarab".
The golden scarab is a beetle called Cetonia Aurata, the insect can be gray, copper, green or gold but still metallic in appearance. The insect is present in central and southern Europe. But we agree that the European streets do not swarm. Jung will then interpret his patient's dream. He will explain to her all the symbolism surrounding this animal. Indeed, in ancient Egypt the golden beetle was the symbol of rebirth, of a second life. This event produces a shock in the mind of the patient, which allowed her to heal.

Even if the premonitory dream and synchronicity are not systematically linked, the premonitory dream often precedes the phenomenon of synchronicity. To understand these two phenomena, it is imperative to change the way we interpret the notion of time and reality. Time is not something palpable, it has no physical reality in the Universe. It is the human species, which at one point in its history, to facilitate and coordinate its terrestrial activities, decided to divide and quantify the revolution of our planet around its star. So, it is primarily a psychological reality. The example of the golden beetle proves it, in this example, we talk about retro-causality, that is, there is a "cause and effect" link, but a future event that is revealed to Jung's patient in a dream she had in the past. If we accept that time is only an illusion and that a part of us, our consciousness, is out of time, this makes these phenomena more acceptable.

Jung's farewell:

Laurens Van der Post (1906-1996), writer, journalist, screenwriter and producer, was a close friend of Professor Jung. He was making a film about the life of Carl Gustav Jung and telling us his incredible story:

" The last scene of the film was to be shot in Jung's house. We worked hard from morning until early afternoon and I can tell you that we all felt like we were constantly accompanied by Jung. It was a dry and hot afternoon, the plan was to go to Zurich to film some scenes and to return in the evening to Jung's house to film the last scene. When we were on our way back, between Zurich and Kusnacht, the blue sky was like a metamorphosis. The sky turned black and we could see lightning. We were back in Kusnacht, we were in the garden of Jung's house. The rain had intensified and the intensity of the lightning had increased. I turned to my camera and was giving details of a similar day that Jung had lived and during which lightning fell in the garden right on the teacher's favorite tree. I had just finished my sentence when the lightning struck the same tree again.

Van der Post will interpret this event as proof that Jung's consciousness was still alive and among them. He assumed that life had simply changed shape and was still part, for some reason, of our space-time.

To better understand the reaction and interpretation of Van der Post in the face of this fact, which the common man would have attributed to mere chance, it is necessary to analyze a premonitory dream that the writer had a few years before the facts. During his time in South Africa, Van der Post dreamed he was in a winding, dark, snowy valley. The wet ground was hardly passable and the snow, which the mountains could hardly hold back, could at any time turn into an avalanche. Van der Post felt that disaster was imminent, when suddenly he saw Carl Gustav Jung above one of the mountains. Jung waved his hand as if to say goodbye and after a few steps towards the sun, he disappeared.

Van der Post awoke with a strange presentiment, when he threw away the curtains of his cabin, he saw a white seagull approaching his window and after fixing the writer, took a sharp turn to flap its wings towards the sun and then disappear. He remembered his friend and his dream. The bird like Jung seemed to say goodbye to him. A few minutes later the waiter brought him his breakfast accompanied by the latest radio news of the ship. He could read that his friend Jung was dead. After a brief calculation of the distance and time between them, Post deduces that Jung was dead when he was dreaming of him. He foresaw the death of his friend in his dream.

Undoubtedly, the memory and emotions of this dream were the basis of what he had also felt on the day of filming at the Jung house years later when lightning struck his old friend's favorite tree. This event reminded him that his friend was always by his side, but for the other team members, it was only a natural phenomenon.

III.8. THE HUMAN PAIR.
KING UMBERTO I.

King Umberto I (1844-1900) was the King of Italy from 1878 until his assassination at Monza in 1900.

On the way to a sports medal ceremony, the King decided to take near the suburbs of Milan, to eat. When the manager of the restaurant leaves his establishment to welcome the royal convoy, everyone is stunned, because the manager of the restaurant looks like two drops of water to the King, but that's not all, after having sympathized with his doppelganger,
The King discovers that there are disturbing similarities between the facts of his life and that of the restaurant manager.

The manager was also called Umberto, he was born on the same day as the King, namely, on March 14, 1844, and in the same place. His wife was called Margherita as the Queen, he had married the same day as the King, on April 22, 1868 and he had only one son named Vittorio, or the name of the prince. Coincidences do not end there, the manager had opened his restaurant on the day of the coronation of King Umberto. The two men had joined the army the same day in 1966. King Umberto I as Colonel and the restorer as commander of the royal regiment.

King Umberto I will be very impressed by this event, by separating from his double, he declared that it was a very important event and the two men, after promising to meet again, parted.

It was not a goodbye, but rather a farewell, because the next day the restaurateur was going to die from a gunshot wound, a friend of his had accidentally shot him while handling his shotgun awkwardly. King Umberto was no better off, since he was going to die murdered the same day, a few hours after receiving the news of the death of his doppelganger.

Some think that the restaurant manager was the twin of the separated King from an early age, others think that the latter was his astral twin, both assumptions could be possible. For my part, I think that there are too many coincidences in this story, to attribute this to simple "chance" would not be very wise. This story, which is far from being an isolated case, gives us valuable information about the implicit order, this underlying truth, which animates us, which guides us and connects us. We are interconnected parts of consciousness and connected to the mother consciousness. It is therefore not surprising to see identical patterns appear, this should even happen much more often than one could imagine in the World. This seems very surprising to us because we rarely manage to decipher them.

III.9. PETER SELLERS OUT-OF-BODY EXPERIENCE.

Peter Sellers (1925-1980) was a British actor, best known for portraying Inspector Clouseau in the Pink Panther film series. In 1979, Peter Sellers shared the poster with Shirley Mclaine in the movie "Bienvenue Mister Chance". During the filming of this film, Peter Sellers was very sick and it required cardiovascular surgery. He told Shirley Mclaine of his out-of-body experience with as follows:

"One moment during my operation, I found myself out of my body. I watched the whole operation. I was like glued to the ceiling and could see every move of the nurses and doctors. I was not afraid and I was perfectly conscious, but I felt that my body had serious problems. Then I got closer to a great white light.

This light filled me with happiness and love, I had a feeling of lightness that pushed me to go further, to cross this light and suddenly I found myself in my body on the operating table, I was very angry and resented the doctors who apparently brought me back to life. I wanted to stay there.

I felt the same sense of lightness and happiness during one of my near-death experiences and like Peter Sellers, I was sad to be still alive. I felt like I had been sucked and stuck in my body. It is a very strange feeling that for me is proof that life continues after death.

III.10. HARAY AND BERLITZ, OUT-OF-BODY EXPERIENCES.

Blue Haray:

This experiment was carried out in the United States, by researchers, psychologists and psychoanalysts, of the University of Duke, in Durham, North Carolina, on a subject called Blue Haray. Haray was subjected to a battery of tests, in which information about his breathing, eye movements, and all other bodily functions were recorded and observed on instruments connected to screens. When Haray began to tell his out-of-body experience, the screens showed very strange data.

It was like Haray was turning into another person. When he began to recount his experiences, the man went into a state of trance, he relived his out-of-body experiences. Researchers also used some animals during these experiments. These animals reacted in strange ways, as if they were confronted with an invisible form of life. During one of these sessions a cat was introduced into the room, very aggressive at the beginning of the session, the cat calmed down gradually to the end of the session plunge into a long sleep. The cat had been calmed by a kind of magical aura.

The most disturbing was the experience with the snake. The animal passed from state to state, it was at first aggressive, then calm, then again aggressive. It looked like the snake was fighting against an invisible entity, probably the etheric b

Charles Berlitz:

This story is told to us by the writer, linguist, specialist in paranormal phenomena and author of the best-seller "The Bermuda Triangle", Charles Berlitz. It comes from one of his many experiences. In 1943, while serving in Panama as a lieutenant, Charles Berlitz had a strange dream.
His mother had just had surgery and was in hospital. The young lieutenant was overwhelmed by the inability to visit his mother. During a break, during a training session, Charles Berlitz fell asleep. It was 1:15 in Panama. In his dream, he was in New York, standing in front of the East River Drive Memorial Hospital, the hospital where his mother was hospitalized. He went to the reception to get his room number and after registering on the list of visitors, he turned to the elevators and pressed the call button. While he was waiting, he had a short dialogue with a nurse who had recognized her through the bedside photo in her mother's room. The lieutenant was apparently wearing a uniform identical to the one he wore on the day of the photograph.
Once in the elevator, Charles Berlitz had a feeling of vertigo, everything became blurred, imprecise, like in a dream and he woke up. He was still in Panama and it was 1:16.

A few days later, he received a strange letter from his mother. The old woman complained and demanded accountability from her son. She did not understand why, when he had come to the hospital and taken the elevator to her room, he had not visited her. The nurse Berlitz met in front of the elevator, had told his mother about the presence of his son in the hospital that day. The old woman insisted that her name was still on the list of visitors of that day, next to her name was noted 12:15, given the time difference between New York and Panama the time mentioned by Berlitz's mother was accurate. This story can be interpreted as a story of "out-of-body experience" or involuntary astral exit. Yet it is proof of the immeasurable strength of the human mind that can interact with matter. Charles Berlitz did not simply make «distance vision», he materialized and interacted with objects and people who were more than 7000 km from the place where his physical body was, and this only by the strength of his mind. If we can travel in space and materialize in another place, present in our current environment in 3D, it would be quite possible to travel through time and space to visit past or future periods of our space-time or even explore those of parallel dimensions.

III.11. JOSEPH FIGLOCK AND THE BABY.

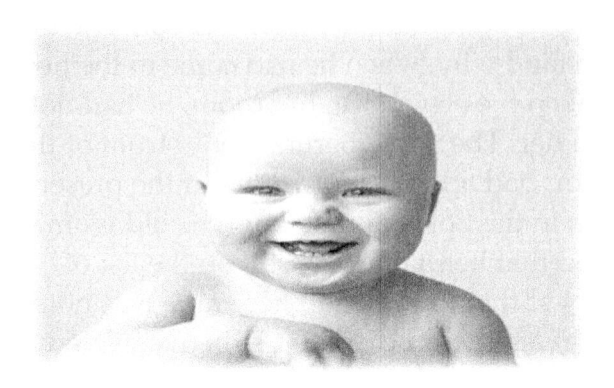

In 1937, Joseph Figlock, a street sweeper from the city of Detroit, cushioned with his shoulder the fall of a baby falling from the fourth floor of a building. The presence of Figlock in this place and at this moment undoubtedly saved the life of this young girl, because Figlock and the baby will get away with some small fractures.

What is strange is that a year later in the same street at the same time, another baby this time a boy the same age as the girl of the previous year fell on Figlock and again Joseph by his presence saved the baby. This story appeared in the daily "Detroit Free Press", and subsequently suffered several distortions.

As if saving the lives of two different babies on the same street, in the same way and at the same time was not enough, we can read in updated versions of this story that the baby that lands on Figlock a year later was the same baby, that he had not fallen from the 4th but from the 14th floor and that the story did not take place in 1937 but in 1974.

There are enough paranormal phenomena in the world, just be attentive and open to this kind of phenomenon. These exaggerations do not help us, on the contrary, they deteriorate the work of passionate people doing rigorous and honest investigative work to serve this discipline.

III.12. THE CURSED CHAMBER.

In 1995, room 311 of the intensive care unit, a hospital in Cape town, the capital of South Africa, was for a few months inclined to a strange phenomenon. Patients hospitalized in this room were found dead every Friday morning for no apparent reason. These patients had heavy treatments, of course, but were in no way in danger of death. After their investigations, the nurses and doctors, finding no rational explanation, supposed a bacteriological contamination of the air via the aeration of the room. The chamber after being checked by specialists, this hypothesis was quickly ruled out.
Meanwhile cursed room continued to kill at a weekly rate.

Following numerous complaints, the police conducted an investigation that lasted three weeks. This investigation yielded no results and room 311 continued to crack down. To elucidate this case, the medical staff decided to constantly monitor the room, and the reason for the problem was observed on a Friday morning at 6:00 am when the cleaner appeared in the corridor of the cursed room, opened the door to room 311 and disconnected the patient's ventilator to connect his vacuum cleaner.

The case was closed and the hospital management said it was considering buying a double-take for room 311 without delay.

According to a 1996 investigation by the Cape Times newspaper, this story is an urban legend, but this kind of story proves that, in most cases, A rational explanation can be found to explain phenomena that at first glance seem paranormal.

III.13. SPRINGER'S BROTHERS.

Ohio 1939, the Lewis, already in a precarious economic situation, are waiting for twins. The family is unable to keep the two children. They will therefore be forced to give one up from birth to an adopted family. Separated from birth, the twin brothers will grow up on their own, without really worrying about the life of their twin. It is at the age of 39 that the two brothers will meet (by chance) and discover, that they have a significant number of similarities in their lives. Jim Lewis' life is almost a copy/paste of the life of his twin brother Jim Springer.
Their case was studied by psychologist Nancy Segal, director of the Twins Studies Center at the University of California,

the psychologist identified an impressive number of similarities between the lives of the two men, we can speak here of two similar lives lived in parallel. To begin with when they met at 39, the height and weight of the two men were identical, they were both 1.83 m tall and weighed 82 kilos. They had been divorced from their first wives, strangely these two women were called Linda. They remarried and their second wives were named Betty. They both adopted a dog and named it Toy. They had a boy whom they named James Allan. They both drove in blue Chevy, their favorite beer brand was the "Miller Lite" and their favorite cigarette brand was the "Salem". They spent their summer holidays in Florida at «Pass-a-grille». The two brothers also have similar tics like biting their nails or leaving messages to their wives throughout the house. Their favorite subjects at school were also similar, they preferred mathematics and carpentry, while they had huge gaps in spelling. All physical and mental characteristics can be explained to some extent by the fact that these two men are monozygous twins, that is, from a single fertilized egg, the same egg and the same sperm. In other words, both brothers had similar genetic information. But how to explain all the other similarities, as in the example of King Umberto I and his astral twin, there is a moment when science and logic stop to give way to the paranormal.

III.14. BACK TO THE FUTURE.

In 1833, a young boy named Adrien living on the Isle of Man had a very strange dream. In his dream, he was the captain of a large ship and was crossing a sinking ship at sea, he commanded the rescue operation and rescued the passengers of the disaster-stricken boat of which his brother Thomas was a part.
30 years later, Adrien really became a captain. In September 1880, he worked for the company «British India». He dropped anchor from Sydney Harbour to Rangoon in Burma and during this trip, he had the same dream he had when he was young but with one exception, this time the geographical coordinates of the disaster boat were also specified. As soon as he woke up, Adrien asked his crew to orient themselves towards the latitude and longitude specified in his dream, which the crew reluctantly did.

Two days later, they arrived at the place corresponding to the geographical coordinates of Adrien's dream and found a boat sinking. As in his dream, the captain commanded the rescue operation and rescued 269 people, including his brother Thomas.

III.15. A LOVE STORY.

Lenny Dean, a university professor, was in love with a woman who was 12 years younger than him. They loved each other, but the age difference was so great that they reluctantly had to separate. It was a very painful separation, but wanted by the couple. Lenny Dean tells us his incredible story as follows: "We loved each other but had to separate. This separation was painful for both of us, we said goodbye in pain and silence. I can't describe my pain in words, it was worse than death. I worked as a professor at a university that was 30 km away. From my home, I started my car every morning at 7:00 to take the Southern Highway and I took the road the other way to go home at night.

I made this trip for 3 years without change or interruption, monotonously. Two weeks after my painful separation, I was preparing to go to work, I was emotionally very fragile and not fully recovered from my love story, I was tense and nervous. I drank my coffee and I remember putting my cup on the table. While I was looking at the reports my colleague left me, I heard a broken sound. It was the glass I had just put on the table that had broken. For no apparent reason. I don't know why, I reasoned like that at that time, but I took it as a particular sign and I was sure of it.

I didn't linger any longer at home, I took my car and started driving towards the university. I don't know when I really realized it, but instead of being on the highway heading south, I was heading north. I had travelled 30 km in an almost hypnotic state. As soon as I realized my mistake, I took the first exit and stopped with great difficulty at the red light of the first crossroads. I almost hit the car that was standing at the traffic light in front of me, and it turns out it was my ex-girlfriend's car that I left two weeks ago. I don't know by what miracle, but she was there in her car and right in front of me. I went to talk to her, and she said to me, "I knew you were working at university today, I was thinking about you,
 I was anxious and tense, I made myself a coffee, I took a sip of it and after putting the cup on the table, the cup broke.

An inner voice told me "it's now or never", so I listened to that voice and took my car. I really do not remember how I arrived at this crossroads, and it is strange that you are here, now whatever the end of our story, I would like to live it with you ".

It is thanks to this series of well-interpreted synchronicities and a little with the help of an invisible force, undoubtedly the energy of this strong bond that united their minds, that the couple recovered together.

III.16. FINAL DESTINATION.

This story reminds me of the film «final destination» in which a person after having a vision of a future massacre, managed to save a group of people. After that, the group realized that a supernatural force was at their disposal "death". Death hunted down, according to a very specific plan, all the survivors of the massacre to then kill them one by one.

In our history, we are not talking about a group of people; we are talking about a single person, who premeditated, prepared for his future death. The story takes place in San Francisco on March 23, 1994, the person who plays the main role in this story is named Ronald Opus.

Ronald, after writing a farewell letter, explaining at length the reasons and manner of his future death, dropped from the 10th floor of the building he lived in. Ronald did not crash on the ground, as he had planned, but instead landed on the safety net exceptionally placed that day, on the 8th floor by the tile washers. Even if at first glance Ronald seems lucky to have bounced on this net, he will not be able to escape death for all that, because on the 8th floor, an old couple quarrels just at the same time. The old man shoots his hunting rifle at his wife, he misses his target and the bullets cross the window to go to lodge in the skull of Ronald Opus. An investigation is conducted by the police and the medical examiner attests to Ronald's shooting death. The old man defends himself by claiming that he used to threaten his wife with this shotgun, which was never loaded and did not understand why the day of the accident it was. Surprisingly, his wife's testimony also went in this direction. One might suspect here arranged testimonies, to avoid the prison to an old man, who would have accidentally killed a man who was anyway committing suicide; but the case is slightly more twisted than that and its outcome will be through the intervention of a fourth person. This new witness said he saw, six weeks before the accident, the son of the old couple loading the shotgun.

After this information which at first glance seems derisory, the puzzle came back into place. Six weeks ago, the old lady stopped supporting her son economically. Angry at his mother's attitude and knowing that his father often threatened his mother with his old shotgun, he decided to load the rifle, so at the next argument, when his father accidentally killed his mother, The only son would have had his revenge against his mother and the icing on the cake, since his father would probably be incarcerated, he would have inherited the family patrimony. This only son was none other than Ronald Opus himself, the rifle he had loaded 6 weeks before was going to cause his own death, I think there is no better story to define the expression "irony of fate". This case was later classified by the police as a suicide.

III.17. ROY SULLIVAN «THE LIGHTNING».

Roy Cleveland Sullivan (1912 - 1983) was a ranger from the town of Waynesboro, Virginia. What makes Sullivan famous and especially outstanding is the fact that during his 36-year active career, he was struck seven times by lightning and survived these seven incidents.
He became acquainted with lightning in 1942, Sullivan worked at Shenandoah National Park, lightning struck a newly built observation tower and not yet equipped with lightning rod. The ranger left the tower in a hurry and a few seconds later lightning struck him and part of his leg and toes burned.

It was the first and most painful experience he would have with lightning throughout his career.

In 1969, while driving his truck on a mountain road, Sullivan saw a lightning bolt hit two trees on the side of the road. It will be struck in turn, normally the metal body of a vehicle is supposed to protect its occupants during such an incident, because the metal acts as a shield as in the experience of the Faraday cage, but no luck for our ranger, because the two front windows of his truck had remained open and lightning had penetrated from the first window to come out of the second, which had made Sullivan lose control of the truck who then ended his race in a ditch at the edge of a cliff. Eventually, Sullivan will get away with burns to his face and eyebrows.

In July 1970, the ranger was struck a third time. While he was quietly gardening in the front garden of his house, lightning struck a transformer that deflected it towards Sullivan's left shoulder.

The fourth time was in 1972, while working inside a ranger station, lightning struck him again. His hair will catch fire.
It is after this incident that he will decide to walk around permanently with a can of water in his truck. In case it happens again.

On August 7, 1973, during one of his security rounds at Shenandoah National Park, he saw a cloud loaded with his previous experiences,

he decided to move away as far as possible from the cloud. When he finally feels safe, he leaves his truck and no luck for him, he will be struck by lightning a few seconds later, for the fifth time. The lightning will descend all the left side of his body and then go up the right side to his knee, following this, unable to walk, Sullivan will crawl to his truck to spray his burning body with water.
The same scenario occurred on June 5, 1976, but this time during his escape, Sullivan twisted his ankle and after being struck by lightning his hair caught fire.

On June 25, 1977, the ranger was struck by lightning while fishing by a pond. This time, it is his chest that will be touched and what remains of his hair will catch fire for the third time. After the shock, Sullivan will get up to join his truck, but no bowl for him, he will be face to face with a bear that he will drive away with a stick. Apart from the lightning, Sullivan had also fought 22 bears during his career as a ranger.
Roy Cleveland Sullivan is listed in the "Guinness Book of Records" and his «Ranger» hats pierced by lightning are exhibited at the "Guines world records museum" in New York.

III.18. PREMONITION.

David Booth:

David Booth, an office worker living in Cincinnati, Ohio, complains about having the same nightmare every day. The first few days, the man keeps it to himself, but in front of the frequency and intensity of his nightmares, he has no choice but to make it public.
Once asleep, he watches helplessly the same tragedy. He is in an airport where he admires the planes taken off, when one of these planes wearing the American colors, has difficulty to tear himself from the runway. David hears the tearing of the engines pushed to the top.

He sees the big machine hesitate to take off, pitch up and then crash on the ground. The fire catches immediately, he even believes to feel on his face the heat released by the fire fed by the tanks punctured. That's when he wakes up, trembling with fear and sweat.

David will then go to a psychiatrist who will take his nightmare very seriously. He will even call the Cincinnati Airport to report his patient's nightmare. Surprisingly, the airport authorities will take this matter very seriously and will try to guess from the details provided by David which airport it might be.

The days passed, and the details of David's nightmare began to become more precise, this change is as in other examples of premonitory dreams, the announcement that the event will soon take place, but the details are still not convincing enough for the authorities, no airport or aircraft type can yet be identified.

On May 25, 1979, the news fell abruptly, the McDonnell Douglas DC-10 on American Airlines flight 191 to Los Angeles crashed shortly after taking off from Chicago O'Hare International Airport, 273 people died, its 271 occupants and two people on the ground in what was to become the worst air disaster in American history.

David Booth no longer had this nightmare after this crash, it proves once again that we are constantly swimming in an ocean of information where everything is «only wave and frequency», that parallel dimensions exist and that time does not escape this law, because if time were something really linear and palpable, it would be impossible for us to explain this kind of transfer of information.

Helen Tillotson:

We are in 1979 in Surrey, a county of South-East England, located south of Greater London. Helen Tillotson is awakened in haste by her mother, who lives two streets away. Helen is surprised to see her mother outside her door at such a late hour. The old lady is very tense and asks in panic " why did you call me?", "here I am now and I listen to you! ". Helen is in shock and tells her mother that she was very tired after her job, that she entered around 23:00 and fell asleep immediately. Although she insisted that she had not been out of bed since, her mother did not believe her and contradicted her daughter. She said that her daughter had come, more or less 15 minutes ago, knocking on her door to ask her to follow her without question. As the discussion continued between mother and daughter, an explosion of great intensity shook the house.

There had been a gas leak in the apartment where Helen's mother lived, two blocks away, and for some unknown reason the gas had exploded and destroyed part of the house. There was no death, but the place where the explosion was most devastating was Helen's mother's floor. "I have no doubt, if the woman had been there, at that time she would not have survived! "later, said the fire chief. The two women observed in a state of shock, the firefighters who were struggling to put out the beginning of the fire that had broken out in the half-destroyed apartment now, because they had been the protagonists of a paranormal story. We still don't know who knocked on the old lady's door to warn her of the danger. His daughter could very well have done it in a state of drowsiness, but there would still be many grey areas in this story. We are entitled to ask ourselves, how and by what process did Helen receive this information? Premonitions are part of the paranormal phenomena that science still struggles to explain.

III.19. NORMANDY LANDINGS.

The Dieppe Raid:

At dawn on August 19, 1942, the allies attacked the port of Dieppe in Normandy, the port was occupied by the German army. As soon as the soldiers, essentially Canadian and English, set foot on dry land, they were fired at head-on and in a row of frightful intensity. Under this deluge of fires, all attempts to cross the walls of the dike covered with barbed wire failed and caused huge losses.
The allied command will finally give the order of retreat and the operation will remain in the annals as a total failure. More than half of the Allied soldiers who participated in the raid will either be killed or seriously injured.

Nine years later, on August 4, 1951, two English tourists named Jamie and Lee stayed in Puys. The two women complained that they had been awakened by the dreadful sounds of clashes at dawn. The two tourists were in a state of shock, they claimed that the clashes continued until 06:55. Jamie and Lee, leaving their hotel room around 9:00 am, expected to see an apocalyptic scene, but will be surprised to see that everything was normal. They were the only ones who heard these sounds. Here is a comparison between Jamie and Lee's testimony and official military documents:

Army. 03.47: Allied warships begin bombing the harbour and soldiers land on the beach.
J-L. 04.00: Women hear men shouting in a storm, at the same time there are gunshots and shelling intensifying.

Army 04.50: The soldiers are heading towards Puys, no shots are fired from either side.
J-L 04.50: Suddenly a great silence.

Army 05.07: Soldiers arrive in Puys under heavy fire, torpedoes bombard Dieppe and planes attack the houses located on the beach.
J-L 05.07: The sounds are intensifying, they are mostly aircraft engine sounds and bombardments supported back by human howls.

Army 05.40: Stop the bombing.

J-L 05.40: A great silence, again.

Army 05.50: Allied fighter planes face German planes.
J-L 05.50: We hear mainly aircraft engine noises, there are also other noises impossible to define.

J-L 06.00: No more noise.
J-L 06.25: Loud cries that become more and more vague.
J-L 06.55: A great silence, again.

The case will be studied by the "Society for Psychical Research" which is a British non-profit association founded in 1882 whose purpose is to study from a scientific point of view the phenomena described as paranormal.
The association will compare the testimonies of the two tourists with the official military documents, these being incredibly close, the association will conclude that what Jamie and Lee had experienced in Puys was a real paranormal event.

III.20. GOODBYE !

It is not uncommon to hear the kind of story that will follow. Often after the death of a person who is dear to us, the spirit of this person sometimes manifests itself several times, probably to make mourning less painful for his loved ones. These manifestations can occur in various forms. Most often, the deceased appears in the mourner's dream, but can also interact as a form of soothing energy or by simple telepathic message. The following are the memories of a woman who wanted to remain anonymous:

"I lost my father eight years ago. The last time I visited him in the hospital the doctors said that his condition was improving day by day and that at this rate he could soon leave the hospital.

I had just spent five days with him and had returned home to rest for a few days before returning to the hospital, but in the meantime, I had caught cold and this illness delayed my return to my father by several days.
It was afternoon, I had decided to take a bath, I went to my room and I started to fill the bathtub. I reached out to the tap and while I was controlling the water temperature, something weird happened, something I still can't explain and understand.

It was as if time had stopped and with time my brain too. I felt the water flowing through my fingers, but I was paralyzed, I stayed like that for a few minutes. After, everything became normal again, I lay down in my bath, I controlled the clock, it was 3:30 pm.

At that very moment, I understood that my father had died, yet I had spoken to him on the phone a few hours earlier and everything was fine, he was even getting out of the hospital, there was no reason to have this kind of negative thought at that time-But I knew I'd lost my father. I stayed in my bath lost in my thoughts. I was seized by the ringing of my phone, I answered, it was my sister, she told me the sad news, I asked her the time of death, she answered me 3:30 pm, it was the time when my father said goodbye to me.

*

My father and the death of my grandfather:

My father had a similar experience when my grandfather died. A few years before his death, my grandfather had developed a passion for beekeeping. During a visit to check his hives, he was stung by several of his bees. He was hospitalized, his condition was critical, and after a few days he died. The night of his death my father was awakened by the voice of my grandfather. He called him by his name. My father had the reflex to control the time, it was 3:30. The next day, he checked the time of death on the death certificate, it was written three hours and thirty minutes.

III.21. GHOST TRAIN.

In 1970 in Newsbury, Ireland, Jonathan Sly, a street vendor, after having made with his goods the tour of several villages, returned to his car. The sky began to darken and Sly had just realized that he was still very far from his car. As a beautiful summer night dawned, the salesman sat down on a large stone along the road and started a sandwich, he was exhausted and had to travel a great distance. He looked at the horizon and saw a sign with the writing "Station", behind the sign a road led to a kind of big hut.

Sly made his way to the big hut, and thought he could spend the night there. Once there, he noticed that the hut was empty and the railway facilities and the station building were in ruins. He deduced that the station had been abandoned for several years and lay down inside the hut on an old bench. No doubt because of fatigue, he fell asleep very quickly. After a few hours, in the middle of the night, he awoke with the suspicion of having heard a noise. He did not dream, he felt a presence and suddenly he heard a metallic noise that seemed to come from the small adjacent room attached to the hut.

Sly turned to the small room and noted with fright that the switch levers were moving. Between astonishment and fear, he heard the whistle of an approaching train and after a few seconds, he saw passing in front of him the famous train at full speed, with its headlights and all the lights of its cars on. The train lit up the old station for a short time, Sly watched it pass patiently to his last car, then he rushed out of the hut and there, nothing. There was no train on the horizon, no noise, only a deep silence in a dark night. He returned to the cabin to control the switch levers, they were all back to their original position. It was as if nothing had happened, yet Sly had seen a train whistling with its headlights and other lights well lit just in front of him just a minute ago, terrified, Sly ran away from the place.

III.22. PREMONITORY DREAM.

In 1986, when Wendy Finkel (19) died in this horrific car accident, her mother had no need to hear it from a doctor or the police, because this information had already reached her. The facts took place on December 19, 1986, it was a day before Wendy's birthday, with two of her friends Wendy picked up a third girl in Santa Barbara to take her to the airport of Los Angeles. The three girls after dropping off their friend at the airport, had planned to go to a rock concert. They had dinner together later that day, visiting Wendy's cousins near the University of California.

The Finkel family eagerly awaited the return of their daughter, that year her birthday would be celebrated at the same time as Christmas and the whole family would be present. The terrible event took place late at night on the "Pacific Coast Highway", the car carrying the girls had hit a slope and flew into the sea. The next morning, the car was located by fishermen, a 1986 Honda, and then recovered with inside the three inanimate bodies of Wendy's three girlfriends. Wendy's body was missing. Wendy's mother recounts that on the night of the accident, she awoke suddenly with a choking sensation; "I couldn't breathe, it was as if I was drowning, when I opened my eyes and fixed the clock, it was 2:00 in the morning, probably the time of the accident, the time when my poor daughter was drowning"

Although Wendy Finkel's body has still not been found, her mother has no illusions, for her daughter died in this accident, as she had deeply felt that night.

This kind of story is not uncommon, I remember an inhumane experience in the United States. In which the researchers, if one can qualify these brutes so, had deprived a doe of her newborn babies.

The young rabbits were taken miles from their mother and were placed under water to be slaughtered one by one by the researchers, each time one of his cubs died, the rabbit trembled. The mother felt the pain of her babies. This was precisely what was sought during this experiment, we were looking for the link, the energetic frequency, the wave, the message... that is what generated this tremor. This gave the information to the mother, because this link although invisible, obviously exists.

III.23. A LOYAL MASTER.

Joe Benson Goshute was the spiritual leader of the Shoshone, a Native American people. He had a dog called "Sky", a German shepherd, they were inseparable. Joe had become old, he was weak and had vision problems. Sky protected him and guided him on his travels. Joe's health was deteriorating day by day, towards the end of 1962, he felt that his end was near, he turned to his wife Mable and told him that he would soon die. His wife immediately notified the whole family. A few days later the whole family was reunited at Joe Benson's bedside, and members of his family decided to hospitalize him in a hospital in Owyhee, Nevada.
This was against their tradition, the protests of Joe and the grunts of his dog Sky changed nothing, finally Joe will be hospitalized.

After analyzing his case, the doctors found that it was already too late for him and advised the family to take him home for the rest of his life. Benson died shortly after his return in January 1963. After his funeral some members of the family will volunteer to adopt his dog, but Joe's wife, Mable Benson, noting that the dog was already very sad by the death of his master, probably didn't want to add an extra layer of bitterness to the poor animal's, she turned down all those offers to keep Sky with her.

Ten days later, Mable Benson looked out the window and saw a silhouette moving towards the house, she entered her kitchen and put water to heat to prepare coffee for her future guest. She then returned to the window and stood speechless at what she had just seen. Her late husband, Joe Benson was standing at the door, Mable Benson was able to keep her calm and explained to her husband that he was dead and that according to their belief he could not be there. After patiently listening to him Joe Benson nodded and said just these few words " I'm leaving, I was just picking up my dog!". Then Joe Benson whistled to call his dog who, shaking his tail, quickly joined him.

Joe Benson added "I want her leash," Mrs. Benson gave her the dog's leash, being careful not to have physical contact with her late husband. Joe Benson took the leash and his dog at his side and left the house, he took a small path going towards the mountain. It was only after a few minutes that his wife really realized what had just happened, once her ideas were in place, she ran towards the mountain and once arrived on the opposite side of it, she looked around, but no sign of Joe and Sky. They seemed to vanish. The couple's daughter, Avrilla Benson Urban, who lived a few meters from the family home had also witnessed the scene, she said at first having seen her father on the porch of the house, a few minutes later, she had seen him again, this time accompanied by her dog walking in a hurry towards the mountain. Avrilla saw his mother running after his father, and in turn ran to catch up with his mother. Once at his height, the two women sought Joe Benson and Sky without success. Later in the day other members of the family joined them, not to search for their late father, but especially to find their dog, since he was still of this world unlike his master.

The search was unsuccessful. Joe Benson and Sky had been part of another dimension for some time.

III.24. CRIMINAL INVESTIGATION AND REINCARNATION.

We are in India, in the state of Uttar Pradesh in the city of Kannauj, the story is part of one of the cases treated by the famous doctor Ian Stevenson. Ian Stevenson is a professor and psychiatrist known for his work in the field of reincarnation. He sought the truth by trying to interpret the signs left on children by their previous lives. He paid particular attention to the birthmarks of children. He considered them traces of their previous lives.

In 1951 was born Ravi Shankar, a boy with a 4 cm birthmark on his chin resembling a stab wound. Ravi claimed to be the child of a hairdresser named Jageshwar Prasad who practiced in some quarters of the place where Ravi lived. Ravi explained to the doctor that he had been murdered for a legacy story by his cousins. On 19 July 1951, two men had cut his throat, the police arrested two members of his family, who were tried, but for lack of evidence, later released.

Ravi had been to see his former father several times, but the man had not taken him seriously; disappointed by this reaction, he ruminated all day long on the tragic events of his previous life, Moreover, since he did not live very far from his murderers' neighborhood, he could not publicize the case too much for fear of being caught and murdered again.
One day against all odds his former father, Jageswar Prasad, visited him. Ravi did not leave him indifferent, but the hairdresser was not convinced, he did not believe that Ravi was the reincarnation of his late son, not yet.

Jageswar wanted more detail about Ravi's so-called past life. The two men discussed at length and at the end of this discussion, the hairdresser had no doubt. Ravi had been able to provide details about his previous life and assassination that an imposter could not have provided, he was indeed the murdered son of

Jagaswar Prasad. The investigation was reopened, and in the face of the precision and accuracy of the evidence, the murderers confessed. Today Ravi Shankar proudly wears his birthmark, as it is the testimony of a previous life.

III.25. ABDUCTION AND UFO HUNTING.

We are getting used to stories involving UFOs and extraterrestrial entities taking place in the United States, but the rest of the world is also full of them. Recently, the subject has left the sphere of the tabloid media to be treated with the seriousness it deserves. This new approach releases languages that previously dared not express themselves for fear of appearing ridiculous.

The three stories that follow come from Turkey. These are the testimonies of three retired Turkish soldiers, the first was colonel for the army and the second lieutenant general fighter pilot F-16, the third pilot also first lieutenant, but on jet type T37.

Abduction:

In the early 1990s, Feza Güllü, colonel of the Turkish Army, was posted to Istanbul. The colonel and two of his soldiers went to a scrap yard between Hadimkoy and Catalca, west of Istanbul, to check the condition of several lots of scrap for the purpose of recycling them for the army. Feza Güllü tells us his incredible story:

The sky was purple, I checked my watch, it was almost 9pm. Then suddenly the sky darkened and I heard a sound similar to that of a vacuum cleaner, but of great intensity. My beret flew away, I had the reflex to look at my watch that I no longer saw on my arm, the pile of metal that had been collected in front of me had also become invisible. Everything had become blurry and I lost consciousness. The soldiers who escorted me, did not help me during my task, they were content to transport the scrap metal I had selected to our hangars when I ordered them to do so. They were waiting for my orders at the blacksmith's entrance. Two hours later, having heard nothing from me, they set out to look for me. They found my parka first, hanging on a barbed wire. Intrigued by this discovery, they continued to look for me and not finding me at the scrap yard, they decided to expand their search area. They ended up finding me 3 km away, against a dilapidated wall of an abandoned farm, shirt open and unbuttoned.

An important detail to note, despite the fact that this place was muddy, I had no trace of mud, neither on my boots nor on my clothes. I initially thought I had mental problems, but after getting a thorough medical test, which is the procedure in the army after such cases, it turned out that I was mentally sound, the only abnormality found on my body by doctors, was that little spot the size of a mole on one of my veins in the groin area of my body. I noticed this spot but it was not harmful and for the two missing hours, I told myself that under the effect of fatigue, I could very well have walked to this wall and then fell asleep. That was the most logical explanation. I resigned myself to believe this until my regression sessions that I realized thanks to the author Kuzey Atacan (author in the field of ufology). These sessions lasted more than three weeks. During these hypnosis sessions, I could not only describe what had happened during these two missing hours and even draw scenes of what was likely an abduction case. I had drawn several praying mantis and I remembered lying in a very bright place with these alien entities. Today, I am convinced to have lived a story of abduction.

UFO hunting:

This is an incredible experience lived by Lieutenant General Erdogan Katakus on May 4, 1983 with 7 of his companions.

"A beautiful spring night, we took off from Istanbul with 4 F-16 aircraft, me and 7 of my companions to make the flight Istanbul/Adana, via Balikesir, Denizli, Eskisehir and Konya. Either, cross Turkey from west to east. Since it was a night flight, the 4 planes flew aligned, in a single line with a space of 2 miles between each plane. We had no problems until Balikesir. At 22:00 we arrived in Balikesir and we took a left towards Denizli. At that time, the pilot of the aircraft flying in 4th position mentioned seeing strange luminous objects and asked me for instructions. I asked him to wait while I contacted the Balikesir airport control tower. I initially thought it was a military or civilian plane that was asking for help, but the tower confirmed that there was no flight planned except ours.

The same pilot later reported to me that he could now clearly see the objects and that they did not look like planes. He asked me for permission to pick up and go check on those flying objects. I asked him to wait. The flying objects approached his plane and my colleague turned off his lights. Then the UFOs were at the height of the plane number 3 which was the same, then the plane number 2 carried out the maneuver. It had been 15 minutes that we were busy trying to decipher the nature of these luminous objects, when I saw appear on my right a yellow light beam, I did like my companions, I turned off my lights, then the light beam passed to my left and gave way to 5 multicolored objects. After a lightning acceleration, the 5 UFOs left my field of vision.

I informed the Konya control tower of the anomaly, the air traffic controllers were amazed, because the UFOs had just passed on the tower. After a thorough investigation we found that these UFOs had been observed tonight by the control towers of Istanbul, Ankara and Konya. It was a strange experience, these objects looked like nothing known on Earth and their behavior seemed to go against all the laws of conventional physics. We made a report and sent it to NASA.

UFO Hunting 2:

On August 29, 2001 at 12:30 pm, First Lieutenant Pilot and Instructor Ilker Dinçer took off from Izmir Military Base with one of his students aboard a T-37 Jet for a training flight. They followed the routine exercises until they saw a strange object in the sky. Dinçer trying at the same time to overcome his shock will describe the object thus to his central:

'We are facing an unusual situation. We are facing a very bright object flying at very high speed, which looks like something between a funnel and a disc "
The instructor then asked the plant to identify the object on radar and began to maneuver around it. A few seconds later, the base responded:

"We have identified great mobility on your plane. However, no second object can be detected around"

After this information the first lieutenant steered the plane towards the UFO, according to his statement the UFO did the same. The UFO approached the wing of the T-37 and the two aircraft began to fly side by side.
Dinçer described the basic situation as follows:

"The object is approaching my wings. It has passed behind us! I will try to take it in front of us! Now it is in front of us! Looks like he's trying to position himself for an air fight."

For nearly half an hour, the T37 and the UFO will carry out air combat maneuvers, until the object, after a lightning acceleration, disappears in the horizon.

III.26. NORFOLK REGIMENT.

The example that follows perfectly illustrates an involuntary introduction into a natural inter-dimensional portal.

Ottoman Empire, 1915, during the First World War, during the Battle of Dardanelles, also called the Battle of Gallipoli, the Ottoman Empire was opposed to British and French troops in the Gallipoli peninsula in present-day Turkey from 18 March 1915 to 9 January 1916. The battle lasted almost nine months and resulted in a total of half a million deaths. The battle ended in the victory of the Ottoman army. After the battle, the British army killed 34,000, 27,000 bodies were found and identified.

7,000 bodies are missing and of those missing dead soldiers, 267 disappear in a very strange way.

It is August 12, 1915, the British army landed for two days faced fierce resistance and could only advance 900 meters in the lands of the Sultan. It is in this context that the 267 soldiers of the 5th Royal Norfolk Regiment, who left as a scout, and whose mission was to invest a strategic hill, began their march, and in the afternoon, before the eyes of the 22 New Zealand engineers. The Zeeland Regiment of 267 soldiers began their ascent from the hill they were ordered to invest, the hill that a thick mist had just covered. The cloud remains static until the last of the soldiers enters it, then takes height to move away and disappear. 3 of the 22 New Zealand soldiers will mention it in their reports. Private F.Reichard number: 4/165, Private R.Nevnes number: 4/416 and Private J.L Newman number unknown.

III.27. ARCHAEOLOGICAL EXCAVATION IN TARSUS.

Before getting to the heart of the matter, a quick reminder of the history of this city of Anatolia is necessary, because Tarsus (Tarsus in Turkish) is not a harmless city. It has over 6000 years of history and has been an important place for many civilizations throughout the centuries. A fortified village dating from the Neolithic was discovered there, the city is of Hittite origin (Tarsa), it was in turn Assyrian, Persian, Greek, Roman, Byzantine, Arabic, Armenian, Ottoman and to finish Turkish. Mark Antony established his capital there during the second triumvirate, Cleopatra stayed there, it is the birthplace of Saul of Tarsus who would later be known as Paul of Tarsus in other words Saint Paul, one of the major figures of Christianity.

The city housed one of the first Christian churches and will hold three ecclesiastical councils in 431, 435 and 1177. It is also a former bishopric.

All these civilizations have left vestiges, treasures and monuments. The most famous and coveted is that of Dakyanus. Dakyanus was a pagan Roman governor known for amassing enormous wealth and persecuting Christians, he is the pagan king of the Koranic episode of the cave people (the seven sleepers).

Tarsus is also known for its underground cities. The modern city overlooks two types of underground cities. The ancient cities buried Assyrian, Persian, Greek and Roman to which is added a series of galleries and underground cities older than 6000 years, similar to the underground city of Derinkuyu located in Cappadocia. As a result, the city is a real "Eldorado" for treasure hunters, traffickers and smugglers of historical artifacts.

An important detail must be mentioned on the speleological topography of the city. In Tarsus, many houses have access, via their cellars, to cities and underground galleries.

The first owners of these houses, after having explored parts of these galleries, condemned these accesses for obvious security reasons.

It is said that these underground galleries and cities are interconnected, so an underground path would exist, starting from the Sphinx of Romania of the Bucegi Mountains passing through Istanbul under the Basilica of Hagia Sophia and basilic cisterns, connecting the many underground cities of the Anatolian plateau to Tarsus.

The Anatolian plateau that can also be assimilated to the ancient Phrygia, country of king Midas, which had an incredible number of underground cities such as the village of Han near the ancient city of Dorylée (Eskisehir) or Nevsehir the underground cities of Derinkuyu, Kaymakli and Saratli to name but a few, because only in Cappadocia has been identified more than 200 underground cities of which only 5 are accessible to the general public. These cities are surprisingly all built on the Ley lines, and seem to follow the planetary energy network. An underground road could therefore exist linking Tarsus to Shambala minor, which is located under the mountains of Tibet, to Shambala which is located under the Gobi desert in Mongolia, to Baghdad and the Giza plateau.

To return to the search, the exact place having been searched is in the district of "82 évler", it is a block of 4 houses that have a garden of 150 m² in common. The garden is located on a large cavity giving access to the underground network. The block was surrounded by barbed wire, framed by large signs and protected by tarpaulins. Snipers were stationed on the roofs of nearby houses and on the ground, soldiers armed with long guns accompanied by agents of the Turkish intelligence services stood guard 24/24 and 7/7. Residents of these houses were relocated and no satisfactory communication was provided.

Official version:

According to the Turkish Presidential Communication Center, the excavations officially began in October 2016 and would be completed in 2017. Officials do not deny that clandestine excavations were already underway on the site since early 2015. In fact, that was their reason for legitimizing such a security deployment. Let's continue with the provisional count of the finds, communicated by the museum of Tarsus. According to the museum's statement, rescue excavations were carried out on 214 islands inside plots numbered 7 and 8. Fragments of terracotta, roof tile fragments, amphorae and an oil lamp were found; and since there was no longer archaeological furniture as an inventory, it would have been concluded that the excavation work was interrupted. That is the official version.

Now we will analyze together the unofficial version. That of investigative journalists and truth seekers:

As Honoré de Balzac mentioned, there are two stories. The official, lying History taught, then the secret History, where are the real causes of events.

The excavations of Tarsus could have gone unnoticed like most archaeological excavations organized in the World.

The trigger, which made all eyes suddenly focused on Tarsus, was the unusual death, in 2012, of policeman Mithat Erdal. Mithat Erdal was according to the testimony of his wife Sibel Erdal, a policeman infiltrated into an organization of trafficking in works of art and treasure hunters.

Testimony of Sibel Erdal:

"That day, my husband came home from work more agitated and nervous than usual. I asked him about the reason for his panic and he said, "For some time now, I have been infiltrating treasure hunters as an informant. They are digging an important royal tomb. I was appointed by the district chief of police. I report to him everything that happens there. There is a sarcophagus containing very precious treasures such as 32 candlesticks, chalices and coins all in gold. The smuggling police branch raided last night, 7 people were arrested. However, today I saw that there is no mention of the treasure in the police report and the sarcophagus is mentioned as empty. I objected, I went to the chief of police, he shut me up. It turns out they were all part of this network".

Mithat Erdal then showed his wife a CD which he later hid in his room and told her by showing the support " my life depends on it! "

Mithat Erdal was subsequently arrested by the police, his gun confiscated. However, he was released very quickly. 15 days later, his weapon was returned to him, a weapon with which he died the same day. The first police report wanted to classify the case as "suicide". The autopsy report very quickly contradicted this version, the only bullet came from the gun belonging to the deceased, but the trajectory of the bullet went from the outside to his neck. The investigation restarts and the police arrest a «Huseyin», who is a colleague in Erdal. This time the reason for the policeman's death will be even more absurd, according to the police report, while the two colleagues were joking between them, the first had accidentally killed the second. Huseyin was sentenced to 25 years in prison and the case was closed, without any mention of clandestine excavations and trafficking in art and treasure. It goes without saying that this version helped many people.

A second anomaly that concerns us almost immediately is the problem of dates. In the official statement, it is mentioned that clandestine searches had been organized since 2015, and that official searches had begun in 2016,
while the murder of Mithat Erdal dates back to 2012 and according to his testimony it had been a while since the traffickers searched the site.

We can deduce that clandestine searches were already underway in 2011.

So why did the official report mention the dates of 2015 and 2016?

On the night of 15 to 16 July 2016, an attempted coup d'état took place in Turkey. The aborted putsch then gave rise to a series of arrests, a real purge was carried out to find from the state apparatus any person who had any relationship with the putschists. The figures given by the various sources can vary, we are talking about more than 150,000 people on average who have been fired or suspended from their duties in the army, police and administration. This detail is important, because the wife of the late policeman will write to President Erdogan in person to ask him to reassess the situation of her husband who for her had been a victim of this putschist organization established in the police and was to have the status of martyr. It is impossible to calculate the impact of this letter on the outcome of this case, but what is certain, is the fact that after July 15, 2016, colossal means were allocated for the search in Tarsus.

The Outcome of the case:

During the excavations organized, this time by the State, strange anomalies will be noticed by the residents.

We have already mentioned the excessive means of security, employed for a simple search, for example the site of Gobeklitepe in Urfa has a historical value much more important than that of Tarsus, but no agent of the Turkish secret services has ever stood guard in front of this site. Or let's take the example of the magnificent ancient city of Ephesus where excavations continue for more than 20 years, there too we saw neither military nor sniper in the surrounding mountains.

Energy anomalies were observed by residents. For example, the engines of cars stopped near this site, especially those of electric cars. The engines of the parked cars started for no apparent reason. Internet coverage was very poor and unstable, it still is. The internet network is broken and telephone conversations are often interrupted. The national company intervened several times and concluded that the anomaly was not due to a failure of their facilities. The problem was some kind of signal jammer that should be around.

Men equipped with combinations of professional intervention against nuclear radiation or other radioactive contamination as well as drilling vehicles of all sizes such as tunnelling machines were seen several times on the site.

The mayor of Tarsus and an opposition MP were repeatedly turned away at the entrance of the site. The staff of the Turkish National Intelligence Agency posted in front of the site made it clear to them that their accreditation levels were not sufficient to know more about the subject.

The writer Haluk Ozdil, author of many books in the field of investigative literature conducted his own investigation and found two archaeologists and several local residents who testified on condition of anonymity.

Archaeologist 1:

This archaeologist had participated in so-called clandestine excavations before 2016, that is to say before the aborted coup and the great purge that followed it took place. He claimed to work for an international group in which Israelis, Americans and English were present and when he first entered the tunnels leading to this strange object, he crossed an area where bodies lay on the ground, A total of 4 corps, it assumed that a score between several agents belonging to the secret services of several countries had occurred there. He did not want to say more about it. He then claimed that they were several archaeologists in the group and that he and one of his colleagues had been hospitalized because of the signal emitted by the device that he compared to a kind of hum. After being hospitalized, the archaeologist did not want to return and was forced and threatened by this international structure to resume the excavations.

Archaeologist 2:

The second most loquacious archaeologist claims that they went through areas where gold objects lay on the ground and that apparently no one paid attention, because the purpose of the excavation was to arrive in the room where there was a strange machine that emitted a signal at a regular frequency, according to him the function of this machine is always a mystery. The machine sometimes emitted very disturbing sounds and it was necessary to quickly move away from it when it began to emit these harmful signals. He claimed that one of his colleagues, after being exposed, had to be hospitalized. He had been deafness and was bleeding from the nose and ears.

I saw this machine that looked like a metal container 2.8m long and 2.5m wide by 2m high, with inside a smaller rectangular box emitting indecipherable signals.

Local Resident 1:

One of the inhabitants of the neighborhood turned out to be a reader of Haluk Ozdil and offered to testify to him of the strange facts that were taking place for several years in his neighborhood. He began by mentioning, like all the other residents, the electromagnetic anomalies of the neighborhood and the inability of the authorities to remedy them. He went on to list the incredibly high number of road subsidence that had occurred in recent years in Tarsus. He also pointed out that clandestine excavations and treasure hunts were part of the daily life of the region and that it had become a rather commonplace thing for local residents. His family, like many other families living in Tarsus, had several proposals for collaboration with art dealers and foreign treasure hunters, but systematically refused them.

He also reported a very strange and very popular story in Tarsus that took place in 2010, concerning a team of workers and archaeologists who entered a cavity below the Temple of "Donuktas" a Roman temple dedicated to Jupiter dating from the second century, to never come out again. This team, composed of 15 people, would have simply disappeared. The search teams found neither their bodies nor their tools.

According to residents, an interdimensional portal is still active in Tarsus and this machine could be the key.

Local Resident 2:

An old resident reminded the author of an old rumor about a machine buried in Tarsus by Gestapo agents towards the end of the Second World War. When Adolf Hitler began to understand that he probably would not win the war, he ordered the Gestapo agents to dig up the machine that was buried in Austria to bury it in a safer place (Tarsus). Turkey remained neutral during the Second World War and the special relationship between the Ottoman Empire and the Empire of Germany before and during the First World War certainly played a role in the choice of the German Führer. This machine seems to be part of the extraterrestrial technological arsenal that the Nazis recovered on many UFOs spit in Europe during their reign. Gestapo agents buried the machine in Tarsus, in a valley adjacent to the city, and left Turkey to embark on a boat in Greece to Argentina. Rumor has it that these agents never made it to Argentina because their boat would have sunk. The story became an urban legend and then was forgotten.

The city of Tarsus has grown a lot since the 1940s and the machine that was buried at the base far from the city is now buried under a block of houses.

Local Resident 3:

This person testified that the excavation work was so well supervised that even the trucks loaded with land were escorted and supervised by the gendarmerie to the place where they were to dump the land. This place was also apparently guarded by military personnel. He drew the author's attention to one of the trucks which did not dump its load and which would have taken the road directly to Ankara. The aircraft in question could have been loaded on this truck and is perhaps in a hangar in Ankara. What is even more strange is the fact that after so many years of excavations and anomalies, the site was not opened to the public, on the contrary everything was buried and concreted. And recently, on 19.04.2022, a fire broke out there, probably to remove the latest evidence.

Author Haluk Ozdil concludes:

The writer did not settle for these five testimonies and questioned many people to perfect his investigation which would have lasted more than a year. After gathering enough information on this astonishing case, he will conclude:

'It is impossible to know exactly what really happened in Tarsus, at least it did not look like a classical archaeological dig.
There is obviously a strange object emitting a signal that is impossible to decipher. In my opinion, this object could have several functions. The object in question is used either to allow access to a parallel dimension, it would be a part of an unlocking system, as can be seen on the doors of our safes, but with a technology and instructions for use that seems likely to elude us. In this case, the Nazis knew the presence of this portal and the choice to bury the object in Tarsus was deliberate. The object could also be an electromagnetic pulse weapon recovered by the Nazis on UFOs during their reign.
The first hypothesis does not exclude that the object could very well perform several functions.

The object may be currently in a hangar in Ankara in the hands of the Turkish army or could still be in Tarsus, since the electromagnetic anomalies continue in the neighborhood in question. This would also explain why the cavity was closed with reinforced concrete. After an excavation that would have lasted more than six years (if we calculate since the clandestine excavations of 2011), the site will not finally be open to the public and all this noise would have been made for some ceramics and an oil lamp.

III.28. THE MONTAUK PROJECT.

The Montauk project is the continuation of the Philadelphia project (1943) which consisted in teleporting a military ship with its crew. This project was also the continuation of another project called "Rainbow".

The project "Rainbow" (1940) is the first successful attempt to teleport a military ship under the direction of Nikola Tesla. It was this success that encouraged the military to go further, to conduct a test with a crew on board. The boat will disappear and reappear a few hours later. At first sight the teleportation seemed to be a success, but multiple malfunctions will be noticed later as the fact that some crew members, by re-materializing, remained stuck in the hull of the boat, others will be taken insane, still others will burn from the inside and finally some soldiers will simply be missing. Scientists like Nikola Tesla and Albert Einstein were part of the team and both stopped the collaboration. Tesla felt that he had nothing to contribute to the project and Albert Einstein feared that with this technology, the military would create a black hole and no longer want to contribute to it. Apart from the experience of the boat, other less known experiments will be carried out in the laboratory, such as the teleportation of small objects, which will result in successes, on the other hand the experiments involving humans will end each time in a negative way, for example, in one of them, humans who should have been teleported beyond a wall will by accident materialize in the wall and die crushed inside it.

Going back to the Philadelphia experience, after this partial success for some or total failure for others, the results will be communicated to Congress to request additional funds to improve the project. The answer of the Congress will be a categorical no, the project is considered too expensive and especially dangerous, especially since the project of teleportation was not the only project under development by the United States during the Second World War, indeed, it was in competition with the Manhattan project.

Congress will vote for the Manhattan project, which will have the green light and the budget necessary to develop the atomic bomb. We know the rest...

The teleportation project should therefore have been abandoned, except that the two generals in office did not see it with this eye. The project will be officially abandoned, but will continue to exist, simply by changing its name, the Philadelphia project will become the project «Montauk». It will be developed exclusively by the army in a kind of semi-clandestine. That is to say, it will not be approved by Congress, which will not allocate any official budget, but it will somehow be tolerated and left in the hands of the military. But the development of such a project required enormous resources, and the military lacked them. So we are entitled to ask ourselves, by what kind of miracle the military would have obtained the money necessary to continue developing this project.

A correlation is made by some truth seekers with the story of a train filled with gold belonging to the Nazis, found in France in 1943 by the American army and the development of the project «Montauk». No communication was made on this spoils of war which was undoubtedly the basis of the development of the project.

A research institute will be established on Long Island near the village of Montauk integrated into a military base, recognizable by its giant radar, the "Camp Hero Radar tower". This military base is located in a park "Camp Hero State Park" whose basement is full of laboratories and tunnels.

The same period also saw an impressive number of disappearances of children and homeless people in the region from Washington D.C to Rhodes Island via New Jersey, New York and Connecticut. These people were undoubtedly used as guinea pigs, given the dangerousness of the experiments carried out at Montauk, it would not be surprising that the scientists needed a large number of samples.

The park was only recently opened to the public (18 September 2002). The military base and the project inspired the producers of the famous series "Stranger Things". Although in «Stranger Things» it is more about experiments on the «MK Ultra» while the project in question in Montauk deals with teleportation and time travel.

This project will change its name again and will be named to finish the Phoenix project.

The testimony that follows is that of Alfred Bielik, one of the survivors of the Philadelphia experience. It is taken from his speech at the MUFON (Mutual UFO Network) conference of January 13, 1990 that I translated and lightened, because fully transcribed, the testimony takes more than 100 pages.

The full testimony can be found here: http://www.bielek-debunked.com/MUFON_Int.html

The genesis:

"My name is Alfred Bielek, I am a survivor of the Philadelphia Experiment. The experiment actually originated in 1931-32, in a strange windy little town called Chicago, Illinois. At that time, there had been, through the 1920s and early 1930s, a lot of speculation in popular literature, that is, popular scientific literature like "Popular Science", "Popular Mechanics", "Science Illustrated", on subjects of invisibility, the attempts to make disappear an object, a person, or the teleportation. I guess the writers at the time thought we might be close, in terms of scientific achievement, but there was a lot of speculation and very little, if anything, had been done about it. At that time in '31, some people decided it might be time to do something and they got together at the University of Chicago. The three main people were Dr. Nikola Tesla, Dr. John Hutchinson and the Dean of the University of Chicago, later Dr. Kirtenauer, who was an Austrian physicist, who came from Austria and was part of the staff of the University of Chicago, joined them, they did a little research and a feasibility study, in fact, they did not accomplish much at that time, during this period. A little later, the whole project was transferred to the "Institute of Advanced Studies of Princeton".

"The Institute of Advanced Studies" was an interesting organization. It was not part of the Princeton university system although it was on the university property, it was an independent entity. It was founded in 1933, under whose auspices, or for what purpose,
 I can't really say, other than someone who wanted an institute for very advanced studies, doctoral research, and that sort of thing. Among the first people to join this institute were some very interesting and well-known people like Albert Einstein.

 I will not go into the story of Albert Einstein, because he is too famous, but he joined the team in 1933. Other people joined at about the same time as Dr. von Neumann.

Von Neumann was quite interesting. He was a mathematician physicist, but he was also a real hothead, that is to say he did not hesitate to apply the theory in the field, for example Einstein did not. There was also David Hilbert.
 Probably none of you have ever heard of David Hilbert. Doctor of mathematics, he was considered in Europe as one of the most eminent mathematicians, he was the first man to mathematically define multiple realities, multiple space and what all this meant from the point of view of a mathematician.

For most of us, it makes almost no sense, and for the average person, it makes no sense, but it's important for the physicist and for a mathematician, because he laid the foundation for what became the Philadelphia experiment.

The Rainbow Project:

In 1933, Roosevelt became president of the United States. He called his old friend Nikola Tesla in Washington and said, "Would you like to work for the government? And Tesla said, "Yes". He ended up being the director of what would later become "the Philadelphia Project". And that's how Tesla got involved in this project. He was appointed by the President as Chief Executive Officer.
In 1936, there was a first hardware test, and this was a moderate success. This meant a partial invisibility, encouraging enough to show they were on the right track, and the Navy was very interested; in fact, they were interested from the beginning in 1931 and provided funds for research. And in 1936, they increased those funds and the project grew. It wasn't the only project going on at the institute. There were other people doing various things. The only man who knew everything about it was of course Dr Einstein who was considered the General. If you had a problem, you went to see the General. He was a consultant for everyone, regardless of the project.
I didn't really understand how I got involved, at this stage of the project, I haven't really entered it yet. I got in a little later.

Bielik takes a break to show the first part of the movie "the Philadelphia experiment". The film, produced by EMI Thorn Corp. of England in 1983, was released in the United States in 1984.

About three days before the film's release, EMI Thorn received a letter from the US government saying "we do not want this film to be screened in the US". They decided after some deliberation to ignore the letter, because they had already made their release dates, and they probably thought that three days before the release of the film, they could play the card of «we never received the letter». So, they released the film, and it was shown in various places; New York, Philadelphia, if I understood correctly, there were huge queues to see it in other cities like Phoenix, Sedona, Arizona, Chicago, Los Angeles too.

Another letter arrived at EMI Thorn in England shortly after - more severe this time, "We don't want this film to be broadcast in the US." EMI Thorn couldn't ignore the second letter. So, they responded to the government and said "if you want this film to be stopped, you will have to get an injunction from the court to stop it". And the American government said, "We will," and they did.

They obtained a court order prohibiting the broadcast of this film in the United States. This court order came into effect in early September and the film disappeared completely for two years. Meanwhile, EMI Thorn went ahead and decided that they wanted to fight it, and they did it successfully. Two years later, a counter-injunction was issued, prohibiting the first, and the film became available again as a videotape.

The film "The Philadelphia Experiment" is relatively accurate and remains true to reality in the first part of the film, until the two soldiers jump from the ship. Unfortunately they wanted to embellish the end to make it a love story, and they distorted some parts of it.

Mr. Bielek goes on to say that the date of the experiment mentioned in the film should have been August 12, 1943.

Now, as I said, in 1936 they had a moderate degree of success. The initial intention was to produce an invisibility field around an object.
So, they continued to work and in 1940, they achieved their first real success under the direction of Tesla, at the Brooklyn shipyard.

It was a small unmanned vessel. The special equipment was installed on that vessel. It was powered by two adjacent ships on each side, to provide cable power; in case of problems, they could cut the cables or sink the ship.

The experiment was a total success, the small ship had become invisible, there was no one on board at this stage, because it was planned for a later part of the test. Well, it was declared a "success". The navy was delighted, they felt that they had mastered this new technology and injected a considerable amount of money into the research of the project and classified it in September 1940, calling it «Project Rainbow». Things moved up a gear from that point on.

Alfred Bielik enters the scene:

Now, I think at this point I should explain to you how we joined me and my brother in the project.

I was born on August 4, 1916, in the New York area, to a Mr. Alexander Duncan Cameron, my parents were not married, based on the little research we were able to do. My father apparently had a rather uneventful, even pleasant, life because he came from a fairly wealthy family. My brother was born in May 1917. And we kept our little guy going. I had a good time, I had no money issues. Came the years of depression (1923 the great depression economic crisis), we decided to go to school and receive an education. My brother went to the University of Edinburgh, Scotland, until he graduated in 1939, in the summer of 1939, so he got his doctorate in physics. I went to Princeton, for my bachelor's and master's, then to Harvard for my doctorate.

In September 1939, because of my father's arrangements, who apparently had a lot of influence in the navy, he had agreed that we would join the Marines, and we both did in September 1939.

We then went to a special naval training school in Providence, Rhode Island, for 90 days. We were probably among the first of what they later called the "Wonders of 90 Days" in the Navy. In 90 days, after taking officer training, you were supposed to know everything. Anyway, it was late 1939, early 1940. We were assigned to the institute. Specifically on the board of the institute, our job was to represent the interests of the navy in this project. They wanted two people who had the scientific background and the military background to accurately account both theoretically and practically for what was going on and what was being done. And that was our main job. We were assigned to the institute; we also had offices at the Philadelphia shipyard. In 1940, as I said, there was a successful trial. The project was closed. Tesla received unlimited funding, as well as the group that continued to grow. I don't remember all the people involved, but we had another infrastructure that came about, a navy structure with the Office of Naval Engineering at the top. At that time they didn't have a naval research office. It was the Office of Naval Engineering, Admiral Hal Bowen. He was not only the overseer of this project, but of all projects of a technical development nature during the war. By the way, this office was abolished in 1946 and replaced by the Office of Naval Research, of which Hal Bowen again served as director until his retirement in 1947. But during that time, he was, one might say, the Top Dog of the Navy.

Under him there were other people. There was a layer set up by commanders. I won't go into the details, but there was a Lieutenant-Commander, Alan Batchelor, who became a kind of team leader and took care of the staff who were to work on the invisibility project.

Alan Batchelor is still alive; he is retired from the Navy. He retired as Lieutenant-Commander. I know him personally. I didn't know for a very long time that there were survivors besides me, and then suddenly I discovered this gentleman through other friends in New York and I talked with him, I finally went to visit him. And I can tell you that he remembers almost every project.

But back to the main topic, the next step in the project was to develop a special team. This was done a little later. In January 1941, the Navy decided that my brother and I needed sea service, so they transferred us to the Brooklyn shipyard, and about a month later, we were posted to the "Pennsylvania," with an old-fashioned combat car, and we went to the Pacific.

We were there most of the year 1941. Around October 1941, when the "Pennsylvania" was brought to Pearl Harbor for some repairs, we took a leave and finally went to San Francisco.

We had a ball in San Francisco at that time, but we were there during this period of October, late October, early November; and in November it was finally decided to return to Pearl Harbor. Our orders were cut off and on December 5, we were on the runway to have the aircraft from the naval air base sent back to Pearl Harbor when we were intercepted by a naval captain and we spoke to him,

and he tells us:

"Your orders are cancelled. Come with me."

We followed him into a room upstairs at the naval air base and were greeted by Hal Bowen, who said:

"Gentlemen, your orders have been cancelled. You should also know that we will be at war with Japan within 48 to 72 hours. We expect them to attack Pearl Harbor. You're far too valuable to be sent back to Pearl Harbor; you'll stay here in the San Francisco area. You can do paperwork. You can finish your year here. You will then be sent back to the institute to continue your work. Enjoy it while you can, because you won't have a break once you get there."

The Tesla period:

Much had changed in the meantime. Tesla had been entrusted with a battleship by a friend of his. I think it was Franklin Delano Roosevelt of the White House. He said:

«You can have this ship; go ahead, make it invisible».

He was convinced that Tesla could do it. He therefore proceeded to build the equipment in several parts, three RF transmitters, and a main generator and two secondary generators. The general plan of attack, without becoming very technical, there were a series of magnetic coils driven by these generators that produced a very intense magnetic field, and initially they were wrapped around the hull of the ship. Later, this was changed to coils mounted on the deck. During this period, Tesla got additional information and suddenly went to the Navy and told them:

'We're going to have a problem with the staff. We're going to have a very serious problem. You cannot develop the amount of power needed to make a large liner invisible without having serious side effects on the personnel.
I need more time. I need to develop countermeasures so that staff are not injured."

The Navy responded:

"You can't. You have a deadline. There's a war. Make it work."

Make it work, in other words. There was a deadline, which happened to be March 1942 and the fateful date was approaching; Tesla was very upset and uncomfortable after this answer. He finally decided, without an extension of time and without modifying the equipment to correct the problem, that there was only one solution for him. And it was to sabotage the equipment, not by physically destroying it, but by making sure it wouldn't work when it was on, and that's what he did on that test date, in March 1942. The battleship had no special crew. He had the regular crew, the switches went off and nothing happened, and Mr. Tesla retired. He said:

"Well, gentlemen, the experiment is a failure and it's time for me to leave. You have a very good element here that can take over and make things work. And it's Dr. John von Neumann, goodbye!".

The von Neumann period:

Dr von Neumann therefore took over, but he too was sceptical and asked for additional time to reassess the situation, saying:

"Obviously it didn't work, I have to go back and find out why."

And he needed a lot of time. The navy had no choice but to give it to him. Most of 1942 was spent with theoretical studies. Around May 1942, they decided they would need a special ship. They decided to build a test vehicle from scratch. So around June they went to the drawing boards to find out which ships might be suitable, and they chose the "DE 173".

In July, they modified the drawings and changed the locations of the two generators, because the destroyer 'DE' was a rather small ship. The vessel, once built, had broken down around October 1942 and then went into dry dock, but it had already begun to be equipped with various equipment. So around January 1943, it was almost ready.

Now, as for "the human equation," what they were going to do for the crew...

Around June 1942, they decided to recruit a special crew. The guinea pigs all had to be volunteers, so the army wouldn't be responsible if things went wrong. The new recruits were handpicked, told they were being recruited for an exotic experiment that could prove to be a bit dangerous.

Well, they had the kind of people they wanted, about 33 people, who were trained at the coast guard academy in Groton, Connecticut. They had about three months of training to graduate in December 1942, and their class leader, their instructor, if you will, was, believe it or not, my father, in his navy uniform. We didn't know what had got him into the army. All the enlisted personnel, including two warrant officers, were then taken to Philadelphia where they were posted and received a second training in which they were given additional details about the future experience.

The crew was available, the vessel was equipped, and some tests began around January 1943, starting with separate systems such as:

1. RF generators and transmitters. While Tesla used three, Von Neumann went to four and finally decided to increase the power of the transmitters. Those that Tesla had selected, namely General Electric transmitters of 500 kw were not enough, Von Neumann boosted them to increase the power of each to 2 megawatts.

2. The synchronization circuits, which were very special, could operate at very low frequency, and were powered by individual motor, to ensure that both generators were in absolute synchronization, otherwise it would not work.

3. A special generator system was built with another very exotic device that had been inherited directly from Tesla, it was the zero time reference generator.

You probably wonder, what is a zero time reference?
It is indeed a term that you will not see in the manuals. It is a system that simply locks on the Earth's magnetic field, the Earth's magnetic structure, and also its mass resonance thanks to a very ingenious system designed by Tesla.

Now imagine all the planets in our solar system and all the planets in our galaxy, these are basically locked into cosmology and have what you call a zero time reference that is the geocentric center of our galaxy. Everything must be referenced to this point "zero time", it is really "The reference". Whatever the local time, you need to refer to this thing for everything to work. And Tesla had found a way to do it quite simply.

Around March 1943, Von Neumann noticed some failures, such as tremors. He did not want to believe Tesla at first, while Tesla kept telling him that there would be a problem with personnel, and he did not believe him. Well, my brother and I believed in Tesla, because we had a lot of respect for him, and we went through some of the mathematical equations and advice that Tesla had left him. We finally agreed with Tesla. We continued to tell von Neumann that he could not activate this system as it was. We were telling him, like Tesla said before, you're gonna have a problem.
Well, at the mention of Tesla's name, von Neumann became very upset but eventually he understood the message and said "maybe there will be a problem".

He decided to add a third generator, so they designed and built one and added it in late April, early May 1943. I don't know exactly where this new generator was placed, maybe it was on the bridge, maybe it was under the bridge, because it didn't stay very long. He had very serious problems with this generator, he could not synchronize it with the other two.

Around the same time, in early 1943, a third man, my brother and I, were chosen to operate the equipment. We were trained to run the whole system because we knew it well and were very motivated to make it happen.

The third man who joined us was a man named Jack, he was a first-class electronics technician, he had the right baggage, but he was just an assistant. Around June, mid-June, during one of the tests, this third generator became unstable and began to generate huge electromagnetic arcs. Jack was hit by one of those bows and thrown onto the bridge. His body was cold. We thought he was dead. He was taken to the hospital, the doctors told us that he was in a coma. Later, we learned that he had been recovering for 4 months before leaving the hospital. After this accident, he never wanted to be part of the project again.

So von Neumann, after analyzing the situation, said:

"the generator is not good, remove it!".

It was removed and we went back to the two-generator system. Von Neumann then scratched his head, we were back to square one and said:

"Well, what do we do now?"

He decided to continue. The navy, of course, was pressuring him. They did a lot of other tests. Eventually, in early July or late June, they decided that the Eldridge (the boat) had to go to sea for testing, which was a normal procedure. So he spent three days at sea. We were in mid-June and everything was fine. They made additional tests and on July 20, they decided that the ship was finally ready for the experiment.
Experience:

Thus, the special test crew was assembled, the captain who was to manage the ship, a man named Hangle, Captain of the Navy, took command. Everyone got on board on July 22, 1943, including me and my brother. As in the film, the ship went to its position in the port and at 09:00 we were ordered to operate a whole series of switches. There were only two generators left at that time, so the film was slightly inaccurate in that regard. So they turned them on and the ship became invisible, from the observers' point of view.

They left it in that mode for about 15 to 20 minutes, and then they ordered us to turn it off and bring the ship back to port, and we did.

The staff, those who were above the deck, were totally disoriented, nauseous, some were vomiting and others seemed to be delirious. After analyzing the situation, the Navy asked to fire the flight crew to replace them.

Von Neumann then knew for sure that we had a problem with the personnel, and he went to the Navy and told them that he needed more time to study this problem, to find the anomaly and to correct it.

The Navy would have said, "You have a deadline, August 12, 1943. You will do the test or you will forget about the project."

They did not take von Neumann's comments into consideration and asked him to meet the deadline. After that von Neumann and everyone worked night and day to try to make the necessary corrections.

The navy decided in the meantime that they didn't want total invisibility. Radar invisibility was enough for them. The underlying rationale was that at that time, of course, we didn't have inertial guidance systems, we didn't have Loran and Shoran global navigation systems. One is low frequency and the other is medium frequency. All you had to navigate was line of sight, eye, and radar. Once the vessel was rendered invisible to radar at night, it was impossible to locate it unless it was optically visible. If it's optically invisible, you can hit an adjacent ship. That was the thinking at the time and they said, no more optical invisibility and Von Neumann said we could modify the equipment to make that possible, and he did.

Came the last day, the fateful day, August 12, 1943. I returned to the harbour. Everyone was a little tense, my brother and I in particular. So we went out on duty, the order was given to activate the switch and turn on the equipment. For about 60 to 70 seconds, everything seemed okay. They had their radar invisibility, we could still see the silhouette of the ship, then there was a blue flash and the ship disappeared completely.

At that time, of course, von Neumann panicked. The ship completely disappeared, he didn't know what had happened to him. About four hours later, the vessel reappeared in the harbour at the same location. It was pretty obvious when he reappeared that something was wrong. They sent a rescue team because they still had not received a response to the radio signals. They had indications that something was really wrong. They could already see it because the antenna superstructure was broken. When the rescue team boarded the vessel, they found this:

Two men embedded in steel bridges; two men embedded in steel bulkheads; the fifth man with his hand embedded in the steel bulkhead, the latter survived but they cut off his hand. Crazy people running around. People appearing and disappearing. Some who were on fire, if you remember the biblical story of the burning bush. There were men who looked like the burning bush, that is, they were on fire but never consumed. And everyone was seriously confused. The only people who escaped this disorientation were those under the bridges, which also included my brother and myself. This is where the weirdest part of this story begins, namely the time journey made by my brother and me.

Time travel:

My brother and I had jumped overboard expecting to hit the water, but we didn't, we ended up in 1983, on August 12, on the shores, if you will, of another project called the Phoenix Project in Montauk, Long Island, at night, inside the perimeter fences of a military base. Apparently, the project was fully operational at that time, we were greeted by guards, watchdogs and a regular helicopter patrol. We were spotted by a helicopter; we didn't know what a helicopter was. The guards came to catch us and took us down into the depths of the facility. There were five levels of basement in Montauk, and that's where most of the equipment was. And we were introduced to Dr. von Neumann. We were shocked, because we had just left him in 1943, he was a relatively young man, and now an old man greeted us as Dr. von Neumann. He quickly explained to us what had happened, rather what was happening, because he had the final reports. That's a long story. How did this happen? And he said, gentlemen, you have to go back and turn off the equipment on the Eldridge; it's already happened according to our records, but it hasn't actually happened in reality, it hasn't happened yet, but you have to go back and do it. We can't turn it off from here.

We cannot close this station; what happened is that the two experiments in time, exactly forty years apart, coupled with each other and created a hole in the hyperspace that sucked the Eldridge.

"You were lucky in a way; you jumped overboard and ended up here."

The other personnel were still on board the ship, locked in a bubble of energy surrounding the ship. He said that "this hyper-spatial bubble was expanding and would create very serious problems; he did not know how far it could have gone if it was not closed. It could have swallowed up part of the planet. There was a lot of speculation; he realized it was something they had no knowledge of, no control over, and they had to establish control by closing the main element generating the fields, and that was the Eldridge. I won't go into the history of the Phoenix project, but you have to know that the purpose of the project was to control time and at that time they had the ability to do so, a total control of time, and they were able to send us back to the Eldridge.
 They told us, you will have to do everything necessary to turn off the equipment, break it if you have to and that is what we did. We picked up axes and broke everything in sight.

211

The electronic tube banks, the power switches, everything that consisted of control circuits and generators stopped, and they slowly slowed down and stopped, it took 3 to 4 hours for things to recover, that is, the vessel gradually returns to its normal state. I stayed with the boat, my brother decided, in fact, if I remember correctly, that he had been ordered back to 83, so he jumped overboard again. I never saw him again so I guess it must be 1983.

The rescue crew boarded the vessel and found the antenna broken. The deck equipment was intact. The equipment under the bridges, in the hole, had been broken by us and they saw the lamentable state of the staff.
They could not bring the ship back to port with such a bad crew. They replaced it with a new crew before returning it to port. They had long meetings for about four days with von Neumann, Hal Bowen, Batchelor and a number of others.
They decided to do an extra test this time without the staff. The boat was repaired and at the end of October they took the ship into the outer harbor, at night she was taken out with a standard crew, and the crew left the ship afterwards. At 22:00, they turned on the equipment and the ship immediately disappeared.

Now, it led to the legends, apocryphal stories of the Eldridge appearing in Norfolk Harbor, Virginia, and many people reported it, it was seen there for ten or fifteen minutes, and then disappeared. Then he reappeared at the port of Philadelphia. When the boat came back, they didn't have to turn off the equipment, it was already off and half of it was missing. They found two missing transmitters, one of the generators was missing. The control room was a smoking ruin. There were no personnel on board to do so.

After this last experiment, the military understood that they were playing with a technology they did not control and decided to abandon the project completely. They sent the Eldridge back to the shipyard, dismantled it and re-equipped it for normal sea service.

Posterity:

After the closing of the project, von Neumann was of course transferred to Los Alamos, New Mexico, as he then went to work with Oppenheimer on the Manhattan project which was a success for him. They had problems too, but there is no need to go into details. And the contest that existed for a few years between the Navy and the army as to which secret weapon was going to be used to win the war, went to the army and the atomic bomb project.

In 1947, the navy decided to reopen the project. In the meantime, there had been a small reorganization of the entire military structure. The Ministry of Defence was created, you had the Ministry of the Army, the Ministry of the Navy, the Ministry of the Air Force, which was created in 1947. You had chiefs of staff, joint chiefs of staff, and of course the large building called the Pentagon. Many people who were present in wartime had retired. A new General was appointed to head the Naval Research office and told Dr von Neumann, let's reopen this project, "Project Rainbow". Find out what really happened, see if there's anything in it that we can save.

So we did it or we started doing it, and then I was called to Los Alamos and a place called Camp Hale, Colorado, and I worked with Dr. Vannevar Bush.

Vannevar Bush led a scientific team to recover crashed UFOs, the first being Aztec in New Mexico in 1947. He also dealt with other cases like the two 1948 UFO crashes. In both cases all the bodies recovered were dead, but in 1949 another UFO crashed.

This one was more or less intact, and they recovered an alien, this time alive. They called it "EBE-1". The alien was wandering the fields after the crash. They captured him, took care of him and tried to find out what was driving him. They were able to communicate with him. They could not determine his gender. They called the doctors because he was obviously not doing very well. He was getting worse every day. The doctors couldn't do anything for him, they didn't know what was wrong. Finally, they called in a botanist, a doctor of botany and found out what was wrong.

This little guy had CHLOROPHYLL in his veins (it's a plant pigment that was found in plants). I remember that it was about three feet high. It looked like the typical image of the little gray, except that it was not a gray. This being had chlorophyll in his veins and he lived by the sun. So, they had to keep him out in the sun, at least part of the time

. And the rest of the time, they kept it a secret because it had very strange characteristics: they discovered not only that it was telepathic but that it was also able to cross the walls. So, they kept him mostly in a Faraday cage.

The alien communicated with his fellow beings telepathically but could also communicate with humans in this way. The being finally died after more or less two years meanwhile he had provided them with a lot of information. For example, according to the information I may have obtained via a former member of the government, the extraterrestrial would have provided crucial information about the "transitor" that will later be used by Dr von Neumann and Vannevar Bush.

He also told Dr. von Neumann about his problem. The problem with the Eldridge, and how fundamentally he could solve it. He did not tell him exactly how to solve it but made him understand what was wrong, he gave him some clues and made him understand that he had to go back to the drawing board and solve some problems and that he could not solve them for him.

Von Neumann did it, around 1949, after doing his homework and much study in metaphysics. Which, if you can imagine a stubborn mathematician forced to study metaphysics and occult issues, was probably obnoxious to him at first, but he eventually became pretty good at it, recognized the problem and started working on it.

The nature of the problem was ultimately quite basic. The ship returned to its reference point, because it had a zero time generator, it was this reference system that brought it back. The zero-time generator had remained intact after the incident while the other generators had been damaged or destroyed, and some other equipment had been destroyed.

And the problem with the crew members was also metaphysical. You have to know that every human is born with his
own "TIME LOCKS".

Simply put, we don't live in a three-dimensional universe.

We live in a five-dimensional universe. The fourth dimension is time and the fifth was not really well defined and named by scientists but von Neumann realized, as some physicists call it today, that the fifth dimension was also time; it is a spinner, a vector, revolving around the first primary vector that indicates the flow and direction of time.

The flow is immaterial. They say that we are moving forward in time, but that is not true, we interpret it this way because of our point of view and our earthly references. We do not feel the time, it is not something palpable, but we can say that it flows at a fairly stable rate and the second vector that surrounds it does not seem to concern the vast majority of the population yet, It's the key to all the secrets around us.

However, every human being at the time of conception receives a set of locks, if you will (this is part of the genetic structure), until that individual is locked into conception, so that individual becomes the homeland of that space-time and "flows". In a way, over time, that is, he is born and lives a life, and is referenced to everything around him, he knows, his friends, his family, his studies… It does not slip through time from a reference point to which it is not intended.

In the case of the Eldridge experiment, the power generated was so great that it broke the temporal references of individuals who were directly exposed to magnetic fields, namely those above the bridge.

They lost their time references. Once the ship came back, that's where the trouble started. As long as it was in hyperspace and the generators were working, they were all contained in the field. As far as I know, no one else jumped overboard except my brother and me. In retrospect, I wonder if we should ever have done that, but nevertheless we did, and the events that took place, took place. When the fields collapsed, the individuals, having until then lost their temporal landmarks, held and contained in the field, began to delirium. Some of them totally drifted from reality, some of them drifted and got lucky because they were standing on the deck because others drifted so far from reality that they finally materialized inside the deck, two in the bulkheads, and one with his hand in the wall, and it was because they had lost their temporal bearings. Some never came back, others had this strange experience of disappearances and re-materializations, several times!
And there were these strange cases these men burning like from within without fire. The navy spent a fortune on electronic equipment to try to fix the problem. In the end, they did, more or less. But everyone was quarantined for a long time.

To date, the navy will not admit that this experiment has taken place. There have been many inquiries into the navy. Numerous form letters were sent by the Department of Marine denying that such an experiment had taken place.

And in 1979, when William Moore and Berlitz wrote their book and published it, Moore estimated that by that time, the Navy had probably spent over $2 million to answer questions about the Philadelphia experiment, with form letters that were sent that still denied that this experiment had taken place.

The Phoenix Project:

In any case, von Neumann did his homework, realizing that he needed a computer to solve the staff problems. So he went back to the drawing board, as the saying goes, at the Institute and developed the first fully electronic computer. At that time, there were no electronic computers. Von Neumann is the father of the modern electronic computer. It is well known and well documented. By 1950, it had something that worked and by 1952, they had a fully functional model, and these books are still on the shelves of the Institute. I spoke with Dr Goldsten, and in 1953 von Neumann would have delivered a new system to the navy, with a computer, with the total correction factors. Apparently, they ran another test with a different ship, a different crew, totally successful, with no side effects. The Navy was thrilled. Of course, the war was over, but they immediately filed this project, dropped the name "Project Rainbow", and reclassified it as "Project Phoenix".

From there, they developed other systems, other materials that go into extremely sensitive areas. I will not go into them publicly, but a lot has come out of them.

Let us conclude with an interesting anecdote that William Moore discovered during his research:

William Moore was researching UFOs. From late December 1975 to early January 1976, he travelled to Canada to meet a family who had experienced a paranormal experience. The night of September 12, 1976, a farmer from the province of Ontario, is back from his field, on the road leading to his farm, he falls nose to nose with a UFO, no light emanates from the object that obstructs the passage.

The UFO is like parked on horseback on the road. The farmer is surprised to see this disc-shaped object on his way but forced to return home, he turns around, to take another path. Once his maneuver is complete, he accelerates and his truck shaves a «ufonaute». According to the farmer's description the entity was three feet tall and wore a silver suit.

After this incident, the farmer's village will be stormed by UFOs, the villagers will make multiple observations every night. It was as if these UFOs were looking for the ship observed by the farmer a few days ago.

Finally, the farmer was visited by three very high-ranking officers, the first was from the Canadian armed forces, representing the province of Ottawa; the second was an air force general, from the Pentagon; and the third is a naval officer from the Office of Naval Intelligence. The military apologized to the family. They told them that what had happened was not supposed to happen, that it was an accident and that they were there to apologize and answer all the family's questions. This was probably one of the few times that officials reacted in this way, according to Moore's account, the family obtained answers to the questions asked during the interview, which would have lasted about two hours and during which the "The Office of Naval Intelligence" would have made a very strange comment. He would have said:

"Oh, we've had contact with extraterrestrials since 1943.
It was after an accident in an experiment the Navy was conducting at the time, on invisibility!"

SOURCES.

1. René Guénon, les états multiples de l'être.
2. Massimo Teodorani, synchronicité.
3. Steven M. Greer, vérités cachées, connaissances interdites.
4. Ata Nirun, Ilahi Komedya.
5. Jaques Bergier, visa pour une autre Terre.
6. Erhan Kolbasi, Galaktik diplomasi.
7. Sirius.org Haktan Akdogan.
8. Haluk Ozdil, kod adi pegasus.
9. William Moore, Charles Berlitz, the Philadelphia experiment.
10. Charles Berlitz, the Bermuda triangle.
11. Ivan Sanderson, article de presse, les 12 vignes du diablesà travers le monde.
12. Wilder Penfield, the mysteri of the mind.
13. Karl Lashley, in search of the engram.
14. Karl Pribram, languages of the brain.
15. Daniel Goleman, holographic memory.
16. Robert Bauval et Adrian Gilbert, le mystère d'Orion.
17. Romuald Leterrier et Jocelin Morisson, se souvenir du futur. Guider son avenir par les synchronicités.
18. Michael Talbot, L'univers holographique.
19. Janet Lee Mitchell, out of body experiences.
20. Celia Green, out of body experiences.
21. Erika Bourguignon, dreams and altered states of consciousness in anthropological research, 1972.
22. Yeni safak efsane avcisi article de presse.
23. David Bohm, a new theory of the relantionship of mind and matter.

24. Michael D.Swords, UFO and government, a historical inquuiry.
25. Kevin D.Randle, the UFO dossier : 100 years of government secretsn consiracies, and cover-ups.
26. La vague belge d'ovnis, rtbf.be
27. Guiness livre des records, Roy Sullivan.
28. Témoignage de Alfred Bielik, Mufon bielik-debunked.
29. Robert Monroe, I'm mor than my physical body.
30. Evans-Wenz, the fairy faith in the celtics countries.
31. Gurney Edmond, Phantasm of living.
32. Hitlerin kavgasi, Ata Nirun.
33. Pascal Dague, les ovnis du III reich.
34. Radu Cinamar, découverte au Bucegi.
35. full testimony http://www.bielek-debunked.com/MUFON_Int.html
36. Photos et images, pixabey.com.

Printed in Great Britain
by Amazon

101 w

AVOID

WORK!

The ultimate guide for lazy, work hating employees!

STEVEN PARKER

Steven Ronald Parker

Has asserted his right to be identified as the Author of this book.

All rights reserved.

Steven Ronald Parker owns the sole rights to his own literature submitted and published in this book.

This book is sold subject to the condition that it shall not by way of trade or otherwise be lent, resold, hired out, have any content removed and used, or be reproduced and/or transmitted by any means or otherwise circulated without the Author's prior consent, in any form or binding or cover than that in which it is published and without similar condition being imposed on the subsequent purchaser.

Ownership rights of Steven Ronald Parker, 2013

A special thanks to Yvonne Rose Parker for the drawings in this book.

Published and Copyright © 2013

ISBN-13: 9781490515878

WHY YOU NEED THIS BOOK

Do you hate phones, faxes, mail, e-mail and people bothering you at work?
Do you yearn to sit at your desk twiddling your thumbs with absolutely nothing to do and yet get away with it?

THIS BOOK CAN MAKE IT HAPPEN FOR YOU!

You can drastically reduce your workload while appearing extremely busy to others, including your boss!
Just follow these tips, tricks and humorous office practices to make each working day a whole lot easier!

HOW THIS BOOK HELPS YOU

This book tells you how to deflect work thrown at you (tips 1 to 78) and how to look extremely busy while you're nodding off at your desk (tips 79 to 101).
The tips are humorous yet practical and can be applied in almost any office environment!

WARNING!

The mistake is not in following these suggestions. The mistake is getting caught.

DON'T GET CAUGHT!

1

ONE FOR ME, TWO FOR YOU!

Be the organizer in your team.

Take responsibility for the sorting and distribution of your teams work.

You can cherry pick the easy stuff, leaving all the crap for the rest of the team!

2

WHOA! THIS IS URGENT!

When someone walks into your department looking uncertain and you're first in line to be harassed, pretend to look confused at a piece of paper, then walk off as if you're going to deal with it.

Make sure that this is not a blank piece of paper and don't make eye contact with the individual!

3

DID YOU HEAR SOMETHING?

Always have your ring tone at its lowest volume, so there's less chance you'll hear it when you're away from your desk, but still in the vicinity.

Your colleagues won't know you're ignoring it... And neither will you!

4

I NEVER SENT IT!

When sending mail, send it with someone else's name at the bottom and PP it.

Any resulting correspondence will be sent to that person and not you!

Make sure you PP with a squiggle, so that it's not retraceable to you either.

5

RE-DIRECT

When a fax is placed on your desk, but it's one that another colleague can deal with, add their name to the top, photocopy and place it back on the fax machine.

When the faxes are cleared again later, the query will be given to the colleague.

6

DON'T WORK LATE!

Wait until the end of the day to send any e-mail that will result in an immediate response.

Click 'send' minutes before leaving, to avoid the possibility of having to stay behind to deal with the reply.

7

PROTECTION

When you are under threat from people 'hovering' and feel that you may be bothered by them, spend your time in a cupboard pretending to look for something.

Cupboard doors provide great protection from people!

8

YOU'VE GOT THE JOB!

In meetings, always volunteer to be the note taker and jot down the minutes of the meeting.

Any tasks delegated to you can be omitted or assigned to someone else when you type up the official minutes.

9

WHY DOESN'T IT RING?

Have your seat positioned near the wall socket of the phone cable.

Pull the phone plug out slightly so that it's still held in the socket, but isn't connected and the phone is dead.

If this is queried, quickly tap the plug back in with your foot and act all innocent!

10

I DON'T WORK SATURDAYS!

When you're chatting with the boss, always mention your fixed weekend plans. For example, you are a passionate supporter of the local football and rugby teams and have season tickets.

The boss will remember this and never ask you to work weekends.

11

NO ONE'S LOOKING

Hide mail that you don't want to deal with either amongst someone else's pile of mail, or between some paperwork on their desk while they're at lunch.

If they do end up bringing it back to you, look confused and ask them how they ended up with it.

12

I'M TRYING TO EAT HERE!

Never, EVER have lunch at your desk!

People will come to you and say 'I know you're on lunch, but...'

Big mistake... You've now got work to do!

13

NO COMEBACKS

When you receive an e-mail that needs forwarding, but you know the new recipient you are sending it to will query the information you have sent, amend the information in the e-mail you have received to suit and then forward it.

For example, if you have chased up a financial report for your boss and the figures do not make good reading, amend the negative figures to positive ones.

Your boss will think business is booming!

14

I'M NOT ANSWERING THAT!

Only answer calls that come direct to you and not those that come through the switchboard.

Direct calls mean that the caller specifically wants to talk to you and is someone you know.

Switchboard calls could be anyone ringing about anything.

Forward these to voicemail and delete!

15

WHAT'S THAT SMELL?

Make sure you always fart at your desk as often as possible.

You will get the reputation of a stinker, meaning that people are less likely to come and speak with you!

16

FAKE GRANDMOTHER

During times of office chit chat and gossip, occasionally talk of a 'made up' grandmother, who is very frail and needs daily assistance from family members.

On the one-off occasion that you are desperate to avoid participating in a big presentation or role play workshop, claim her death and take two weeks holiday, perhaps in Spain!

17

WHAT ARE YOU TALKING ABOUT?

When someone calls with a query and you've got no idea what they're talking about, tell them you know who deals with those issues.

Either give them someone else's direct number, or put them through to the switchboard.

You can make sure it doesn't come back to you by putting your phone on divert for 5 minutes.

18

DON'T OPEN IT!

When you get an e-mail that looks suspicious and you may have to act upon it, view auto-preview so that it doesn't register as 'read'.

If it's something that you don't want to do, don't open it!

You can claim that your e-mail is down, or you haven't had the chance to check them.

19

I KNOW NOTHING!

When someone calls you with a query that you know nothing about, claim you are fairly new to the company, thus giving you the perfect excuse not to know the answer without sounding stupid!

If you're lucky, you may also avoid further questions.

20

VOLUNTEER! YES, REALLY DO!

Volunteer for all the mundane tasks that no one wants to do, like filing, photocopying and making coffee for the team.

You can take your time while your colleagues deal with all your phone calls and people who come to bother you.

You may even get thanked for doing this!

21

WHY'S THAT MACHINE QUIET?

Keep empty fax toner cartridges hidden in your draw.

When you want a quiet day, sneakily replace an existing toner cartridge with an empty one, so that the fax machine will either print illegible text, or not print at all!

22

THEY'LL BE BACK!

When a work colleague is on holiday and you take a call asking for them, don't say that they're on holiday and handle the query yourself.

Instead, say that they've just stepped out of the office and you will get them to return the call on their return, making sure you withhold your name!

Forget the query, as this can only look bad on the colleague for not ringing the caller back!

23

I DIDN'T DO IT!

Whenever your signature is required to prove that you've completed a task, but you've done it wrong, use an illegible signature so that the error is not traced back to you!

Have a sample of your real signature nearby, so that you can 'prove' it wasn't you who signed off incompetent workmanship!

24

STOP RINGING!

When you're in the office on your own and a colleagues phone rings, stand up but don't go over to answer it.

Instead, stand positioned so that you look as if you're about to walk over and answer it, but are quickly finishing off some work on your desk first.

When someone walks in, pretend that you were just about to go over and answer it, but let them instead!

25

I THINK YOU SHOULD DO IT!

In meetings, when a task has to be delegated, make sure that you don't make eye contact with the individual who is issuing the task.

Instead, turn your head quickly and stare at a colleague.

They'll feel pressured into volunteering!

I'M OUTTA HERE!

When someone internal calls you wanting to visit your office and speak with you face-to-face, tell them to come over immediately so that they can speak with 'someone'.

Leave the office for 5 minutes and on your return, the caller will be there bothering someone else!

27

THEY'LL DO IT, FOR SURE!

When you receive work via e-mail, but it has been sent to both you and a colleague, immediately delete it on the assumption that the colleague will deal with it.

You can't be singled out if it doesn't get done!

SILENCE (1)

When there's an imminent threat of people disturbing you at your desk, pick up the phone and pretend to be talking to someone.

You don't have to talk yourself, just nod and say 'yes' 'ok' a few times and they shouldn't disturb you!

SILENCE (2)

When you pretend to be on the phone to avoid people, but they stand waiting to disturb you, simply throw in a line such as 'I'll head on down immediately'.

You now have perfect excuse to direct the person to a colleague and take a 10 minute tour of the building!

SILENCE (3)

When you're on a mobile phone and people are waiting to speak with you, throw in a line such as 'I'll just have a look for you'.

Walk towards a cupboard, or out of the office!

31

IGNORE IT!

When you notice a fax machine reading 'paper jam' or 'paper empty', ignore it and pretend that you never noticed, hoping that no one else notices it either!

32

TAKE A MESSAGE

When someone phones you, either take a message informing the caller that 'someone' will get back to them, or just forward the call to voicemail.

Then pass the message (that you either took yourself, or forwarded to voicemail) onto a colleague as if the person rang specifically for them!

33

WHY'S MY NAME ON THERE?

When faxes or pieces of mail have your name on it, erase your name and photocopy.

Destroy the original and pretend that the copy was sent without being addressed to a specific person, thus taking the responsibility away from you!

34

ONE WAY TO COMMUNICATE

When you have e-mail at work, this can dramatically reduce the need for face-to-face discussion.

If possible, always communicate via e-mail, especially if it's a discussion you don't want to have!

DON'T FEED IT!

When no one's looking, pull the fax paper out slightly so that the machine can't feed it and you don't receive any faxes.

Passers by will not realize the problem!

36

I DIDN'T GET IT, HONEST!

When someone pushes you for your e-mail address, make sure to give them an incorrect address so that you never receive their mail.

When they ask if you've received a message, you can legitimately claim you haven't!

ALWAYS ON LUNCH!

Only ever make calls between midday and 2pm in the afternoon, as the person you're trying to contact is likely to be on lunch.

If you're lucky, you won't have to speak with them and can either leave a message, send them an e-mail or just forget about it!

SHUT-DOWN

Whenever you require a 2 minute break, shut down your computer and switch it back on again.

Take a breather while it's loading.

If queried, say that the screen froze and the computer needed re-starting.

I'M A REALLY GOOD EMPLOYEE!

Appear helpful to work colleagues.

Take work off one fellow employee and give it to another, stating that you have been asked to give it to them.

40

OFF THE HOOK

Spend your whole day with the phone receiver slightly off the hook so that it's not noticeable.

If this is queried, claim ignorance and say that you must have knocked it off accidentally.

Perhaps have a document partly covering the phone so that it's hidden.

41

NATURE CALLS, AGAIN!

Try to drink as much water during the day as possible, within reason!

This will result in many time wasting trips to the toilet.

You may choose to take the longer route to the toilets at the furthest end of the building.

42

PASS THE PARCEL

When you open the mail in the morning and find something that you're unsure of, place it in an internal envelope and send it to someone in another department at random.

Just hope that it never finds its way back!

43

AN ABSOLUTE PRIORITY!

In the weeks leading up to a holiday, put off doing any work that you don't want to do.

You can pass this onto a colleague as 'priority work' while you're away!

GET BACK!

When a colleague is out of the office and they have their phone diverted to you, if your phone rings and it's a diverted call, simply press the 'forward' button on your phone and it should divert back to THEIR voicemail.

You can claim that you must have been on the phone when the call came through and therefore you were unable to answer it!

45

THEY WANT YOU TO DO IT!

When receiving work via e-mail, tell the sender that someone else has volunteered for the task, as it is their area of 'expertise'.

Then tell your work colleague that the sender has specifically asked if they will do it.

THEY TOLD ME TO DO IT!

When you're asked by your manager to ring someone to pass on a message, say that you tried calling, but they weren't in and you have sent them an e-mail instead.

Communicating via e-mail doesn't allow any verbal backlash!

You can claim that someone else who answered told you to do this.

THAT'S GOOD COFFEE!

When you're asked to deliver a package (either by car or by foot), make the delivery and then spend a couple of hours at the local café.

Blame traffic or claim you got lost!

WHO AM I? (1)

Have your voicemail mention your name, but not the department you work for.

People who want to speak with you can leave a message, whereas those who want to leave a general message for the department will not know who you are and therefore be less likely to leave a message.

WHO AM I? (2)

Make sure that if your voicemail does mention your department, you don't include your name.

Any messages left on the voicemail system can be deleted without the caller having anyone specific to blame for not returning their call.

50

I'M NOT DOING THAT!

When someone asks you if you're busy, this automatically means that they want to give you more work!

Counter this by immediately stating that you're extremely busy and would appreciate some help with your workload.

They'll think twice about giving you more work and unload it on someone else!

51

PUT IT BACK!

When you open your mail in the morning and find something that your department deals with, but you don't want to, place it in a new envelope and return it to the 'mail in' tray.

Let someone else deal with it!

52

HOLD THE BACK PAGE

When you receive a fax with multiple pages, destroy the last page and fax back claiming that you didn't receive the full message.

Wait for the 2nd request while plotting to deflect the query on its return!

WRONG DEPARTMENT IDIOT!

When someone presents you with a difficult query, direct them to another department to ask for someone that doesn't exist.

Make up a name and job title.

You can claim confusion later if you are queried about names and job titles.

54

THEY WON'T REMEMBER!

When you are asked by your manager to ring someone, wait until the end of the day and say that you tried a few times, but didn't get an answer.

Say that you will try again tomorrow, but don't, as it will all be forgotten by then!

WOW! I GOT MY HOLIDAYS!

Try to duplicate the printout of an e-mail on your word processing system as it would appear from the e-mail printout itself.

This may prove useful, for example, when forging fake authorization for holidays!

I DID SPEAK TO THEM, I THINK!

Always write down voicemail messages as if you took them as calls and delete them from the system.

This will not draw attention to the fact you are forwarding all your calls to voicemail!

57

TAKE ADVANTAGE OF DEATH

When someone at your workplace dies, always exaggerate the extent of how well you knew and spoke with them.

Appear upset and if you're lucky, you may get some time off to 'get over it'.

Spend a long weekend in Madrid!

DEFLECT AND GO

When you receive a call that anyone can deal with, turn to a work colleague and say that you have a call specifically for them.

Put the call through immediately, so that their phone is ringing and they don't have time to ask you any questions.

Once they take the call, walk out of the office to avoid any comeback!

BETTER TAKE A NEWSPAPER!

When someone comes to you talking gibberish, tell them that you need to go and get some information, but then just hide in the toilets.

On your return, hope that either a colleague has dealt with them, or that they got sick of waiting and left!

60

I DON'T DEAL WITH THAT!

When you're speaking with someone and they want to send a query in writing to you, either ask them to forward it to the general department address, or give them someone else's name as a specific contact who deals with these issues.

If it's someone that you don't know very well, you could claim that you're going on holiday soon, so it would be better off being sent to one of your work colleagues!

ANOTHER MEETING!

During busy periods of the day, put your phone on voicemail.

If anyone complains that they couldn't contact you, tell them that you were unavailable, as you had meetings to attend.

62

HEAD DOWN, DON'T LOOK UP!

In meetings, always keep your head down and take prolonged notes, so that you don't have to contribute verbally in any way!

This is specifically useful when tasks are being delegated and you don't want to make eye contact with anyone!

OOPS! I DROPPED IT!

When the phone rings and someone's there to see you answer it, pick up the receiver with the tips of your fingers and then immediately drop it.

You can hang up claiming that it slipped out of your hands!

BREATHING SPACE

Date stamp mail that you don't want to deal with for a few days after it was received and then hide it, so that you can claim receipt on that date.

This gives you plenty of time to plot various ways of passing the work onto someone else!

DON'T PICK UP, DON'T PICK UP!

When your manager asks you to ring someone to deliver a message or obtain information, only let the phone ring two or three times.

Hopefully you won't get an answer, but you can genuinely say that you tried!

WHO SAID THAT?

When there is an imminent threat of someone coming over to speak with you, become embroiled in some idle conversation with a colleague. Make sure that your back is turned so that when they approach, the colleague will see them first and be obliged to respond.

Whichever side of you they approach, turn the other way slowly as if confused as to where they are, thus leaving the colleague and person face to face.

You can now drift away leaving the colleague to deal with them!

THAT'S IT, I'M OFF!

When you are left in the office alone, leave a couple of hours early and hope that no one comes to see you when you're gone.

Leave a fake note on your desk stating 'just nipped down to marketing', in case anyone does come looking for you!

OOPS, I FORGOT! (1)

When someone calls wanting you to do something for them, ask them to put it in an e-mail.

Say that it's so you won't forget, or that you want all the information documented.

You now have the perfect excuse to forget by claiming you haven't yet read your e-mails!

OOPS, I FORGOT! (2)

Never make the mistake of claiming that you've not read an e-mail if you have!

If you have read or delete it, an auto reply of 'read' 'read deleted' or 'unread deleted' could be sent.

They'll know you're lying!

70

I'M NOT TELLING HIM!

When someone queries something and you know the answer is not what they want to hear, look uncertain and redirect them to a colleague.

Leave the office before they start to complain!

71

JUST SHRED IT!

If you receive mail that only you can deal with, but you really don't want to, shred it!

You can claim non receipt.

72

WILL THEY EVER RESPOND!

When you send a fax and receive a confirmation message that the fax has FAILED, bin the failure notice and forget the query.

You can blame the intended recipient for not responding!

IT'S ONLY 5 MIN'S!

Never tell colleagues when you go for lunch and take 5 minutes extra every day.

It will be hard for anyone to monitor your lateness!

SOMEONE ELSE'S FAULT!

Never give your name when you answer the phone.

When the caller asks for you and you don't know them, tell them that you are someone else and take a message.

Don't call them back, as you can blame the 'someone else' for not passing on the message!

75

GET A NEW SHIRT!

Wear the same shirt, socks and underwear for weeks at a time.

You will soon begin to reek, meaning people will avoid you at all costs.

Some people do this without realizing!

3 MONTH HOLIDAY

Before a holiday, make sure your e-mail 'out of office assistant' claims that you're away longer than you are.

This gives you time to catch up on your work when you return, whilst people think you are still off.

Your 'assistant' should also give alternative contact details, so that your colleagues are sent your work while you're away.

77

YOU CAN'T SEE ME!

Have your desk chair at a low height setting.

It will be difficult for people to spot you hiding behind the computer screen!

AAH! I CAN HIDE HERE!

When you have work that doesn't require you to be at your desk, find a quiet office to work from.

If asked, say that you need to concentrate on the job!

Now that you have dramatically reduced your workload, whilst you may still have some work to do, you will undoubtedly find you go through large periods of the day with very little to do!

But how do you get through this when there are managers walking around spying on you?

Read on to find out...

NO MORE, THANKS!

Make sure that any work you have lasts the whole day.

Don't have the attitude of getting work done to take on other responsibilities.

Managers will assume that you're not busy and give you other tasks, which soon become the norm!

HERE'S ONE I DID EARLIER

Every so often, take a piece of work that you have completed in work time home with you.

Bring it back the next day and consult with your manager, claiming that you have done it at home and want to check it's ok.

You will appear a conscientious and committed employee!

81

WHO'S SPYING ON YOU?

When you're out of the office, precisely position a pen, stapler or eraser over the work on your desk.

When you return, you can tell if things have been moved and someone has been looking at your stuff!

82

SAY NO TO SCREENSAVERS!

Never use a screensaver!

If you fall asleep at your desk, people will see that your computer is not in use.

They may come over to investigate!

BEWARE WHO'S COMING! (1)

Always have your computer screen facing away from onlookers and those who approach you.

When someone comes over to talk with you, you'll gain vital seconds to minimize the website you're looking at to reveal the 'work' you're dealing with!

BEWARE WHO'S COMING! (2)

If you are ever caught looking at a website, claim that it's a pop-up and express your annoyance and frustration at how they slow down your computer.

You could also claim you're on lunch or conducting 'research'.

CHECK OUT MY SCHEDULE!

Have a large calendar wall chart pinned up near your desk, with random dates and weeks highlighted, circled and written over.

You'll look as if you have a 'very busy' schedule!

86

I'VE ONLY GOT TWO HANDS!

When carrying paperwork around the office (which is great for looking busy), split the work in half and hold it in both hands.

You will look as if you are dealing with two queries at once!

LOOK WHAT I'M DOING! (1)

Always have 'work' scattered all over your desk and make sure that this relates to the 'work' on your screen.

If you are queried, you have something to say you are doing!

88

LOOK WHAT I'M DOING! (2)

To look genuinely busy, make up a simple question relating to the 'work' on your screen.

Ask your boss inquisitively when they walk by, so it looks as if you're actually working!

MAKE YOUR ESCAPE!

At the end of the day, pack up half an hour early to ensure a quick escape.

However, do leave some last bits of work on your desk, so that you look as if you're still working!

I HAVEN'T DONE IT YET!

Take a photocopy of bulky work that you have already completed and position it on your desk in clear view of others.

It will appear to others that this is work you still have to do!

DON'T SPEAK TO ME! (1)

When your boss enquires about the work you're supposed to be doing, never be too specific, otherwise they may become interested and ask for updates or progress reports!

Just generalize your tasks in a dull and unenthusiastic voice.

DON'T SPEAK TO ME! (2)

In order to reduce the likelihood of your boss querying the 'work' you are doing when they walk by, turn your back to them, stare confusingly at the screen whilst consulting a document.

They will assume that you're busy on some extremely complicated work project!

LOOK, I'M ON THE PHONE!

At random points in the day, pretend to be on the phone, so that you look busy and are taking calls.

Have pre-planned reasoning for the call, just in case you are asked who called or what it was about!

94

SQUEEZE IT IN

Whenever you're asked by your boss to do something on a future date, consult your 'empty diary' and pencil in the instructions.

You will look busy, efficient and organized!

95

IS ANYONE WATCHING ME?

Spend time repeatedly cleaning out drawers and shuffling documents about.

This will make you look busy!

If questioned, you can say you're tidying and organizing work, which sounds good!

I'M A REALLY HARD WORKER!

Just before a manager walks by from behind (when you see them coming out the corner of your eye), lean back in your seat and breathe out as if you're exhausted at the amount of graft you are putting into your 'work'.

Then look surprised when you see them by saying 'oh, hello!'

WHAT A WASTE OF TIME!

When you're sat at your desk with most of the afternoon remaining and you only have one job left to do (for example, to write a letter), type the letter over and over again, deleting the text each time you've done it.

You will look continually busy to onlookers!

ALWAYS EXAGGERATE

In meetings, always exaggerate the depth and difficulty of the work you are currently dealing with, so that people will think you're very busy and not give you any more!

99

CLICK! CLICK! CLICK!

Make sure that you regularly alternate what appears on your computer screen.

Leaving the same thing on your screen suggests that you have very little to do and this may get noticed by onlookers!

BEFORE YOU LEAVE

Make sure that any work you have completed is left on your desk until the end of the day.

You can give this to your manager just before you leave, making it look as if you've been busy working on it all day.

Alternatively, keep it until the end of the week and people will assume you're snowed under!

101

BE THE BEST, ON SCREEN!

Locate websites that advise on how to become a better employee, such as those that assist with becoming more efficient, effective and pro-active (and other such buzz words).

Leave these on your screen when you are away from your desk, so that passers by (including your boss) will think you are striving to be the best!

10 WAYS TO AVOID WORK!

1. Win the lottery
2. Check your attic for valuable junk
3. Compete on TV game shows
4. Invent the 'next best thing'
5. Marry a wealthy spouse
6. Sue a large corporation
7. Rob a bank
8. Write begging letters to celebrities
9. Grow a money tree
10. Inheritance – Murder your grandmother!

ABOUT THE AUTHOR

Steven Parker studied for as long as possible before entering the world of work.

Despite an enthusiastic start, Steven soon began to realize what he had always thought, that work wasn't for him and set about doing almost anything to avoid it.

Needless to say, this book came naturally to Steven, with the purpose of making working life that little bit easier for everyone.

Printed in Great Britain
by Amazon